FOCOLARE after thirty years

1

Published in the United States by New City Press
the Publishing House of the Focolare Movement, Inc.
206 Skillman Avenue, Brooklyn, N.Y. 11211

© 1976 by Città Nuova Editrice, Roma, Italy
Printed in Hong Kong

The interviews contained in this book were conducted
by Sergius C. Lorit.
Translated from the original Italian by New City Press Staff.
The English edition was prepared by Nuzzo Grimaldi.

Cover design: Silvio Russo

FOCOLARE
AFTER 30 YEARS

BY S.C.LORIT & N.GRIMALDI

Books on the Focolare

Chiara Lubich	Meditations
	That All Men Be One
	When Our Love Is Charity
	A Little Harmless Manifesto
	It's A Whole New Scene
	The Word Of Life
	"Jesus In The Midst"
Pascal Foresi	Reaching For More
Claude Miner	Me Too, Forever
	The Gospel In Action

Contents

Translators' Note:

Throughout the book we have used a few words from the original Italian that have become proper names in the Movement all over the world. "Focolare" (plural "Focolari") is an Italian word for hearth or fireplace around which people gather as a family; it refers here to a community of consecrated people who live the spirituality of the Movement, and it has also come to signify the Movement as a whole. A man who lives in the men's Focolare is called a "Focolarino" (plural "Focolarini") and a woman living in the women's community is a "Focolarina" (plural "Focolarine").

INTRODUCTION

"Can you tell me more about the Focolare Movement?" "How did it begin?" "What does it stand for?" "How was it developed over the years?" Questions like these have come from many, many people who have come into contact with this Movement and who want to know more about it.

This book is an attempt to respond to these many requests for more information about the Focolare Movement. But it should be made clear that it is not intended to give a complete view of the subject. For the Focolare Movement, as a movement of renewal, is continually growing, expanding and developing, albeit from the strong and solid spirituality which lies at its heart.

The book contains interviews with a number of people with responsibility in the Movement at an international level, beginning with Chiara Lubich, the foundress and president. It also describes some of the activities of the Movement throughout the world.

We feel confident that this book will serve effectively as an introduction to the Focolare Movement. Other books on the spirituality of the Movement and, most especially, direct contact with it can provide a deeper knowledge of the Movement.

THE EDITORS

1. HOW IT ALL BEGAN

> *The Focolare Movement had its beginnings late in 1943. Now, after more than 30 years, I wanted to have a close look at this new flower in the Church's garden. It was only natural that I should start my series by interviewing the foundress of this movement, Chiara Lubich, who is also its president. The interview took place in her Focolare in Rocca di Papa, near Rome, Italy.*

The First Intuition

Q.: The Focolare Movement is thirty years old and you are its foundress. How did you get the idea of giving life to this new form of Christian witness?

Chiara: I must say sincerely that I never had the idea of starting or founding a movement. Such a thought was as far from my mind as the East is from the West, and this fact has always seemed most beautiful to me. The idea came from somewhere else. If the Movement is what it is today, one can say that it came solely from God.

Nevertheless, sometimes I have said to the Focolarini who are closest to me, that there was a moment in my life — of which I understood the meaning only later — which could be interpreted perhaps as a prelude of what was to come.

In 1939, I attended a convention in Loreto, Italy, for Catholic students. It was my first long trip away from home. I didn't know yet what the Lord wanted from me but I didn't worry about it.

The first time I entered the little house of Loreto, which is protected by a church built like a fortress, I was deeply moved. I didn't have the time to ask myself whether or not it was historically proven that that was the house in which the Holy Family had dwelled. I found myself alone immersed in that great mystery, and my tears flowed continually — which is unusual for me. I started to meditate on everything that could have happened there: the annunciation of the angel to Mary, and the life of Jesus, Mary and Joseph.

With a sense of veneration, I was touching those stones and beams, picturing Joseph building the house, and Jesus as a child speaking or running across the room. I was looking at those walls that were privileged to have re-echoed the voice and the songs of Mary. Although I still attended the convention, rather than remain with my companions near the convention site, I went to visit the little house every day. And there I always had, with greater or lesser intensity, the same impression, the same deep emotion. It was as if a special grace of God were enveloping me, as if the "divine" was almost overpowering me. It was contemplation, it was prayer, it was in a certain sense like living with the family of Nazareth. I will never forget it.

Then the convention concluded with a ceremony in that

Chiara Lubich, Foundress and President of the Focolare Movement.

One of the streets of Trent, Italy after the bombardments of 1943 which destroyed people, possessions, as well as the ideals of many. It was then that Chiara Lubich with her first companions initiated the Focolare Movement.

same church crowded with people, especially with girls wearing white veils. I was participating in it with all my heart. And at a certain moment I understood: I had found my way, and many, many people would follow it.

I went back home to Trent happy. Nothing else was clear except what I've told you. However, I told a priest who asked me how it went in Loreto, "I have found my way." "Which way, marriage?" he asked. "No," I answered. "To live a life totally given to God alone in the world?" "No." "The convent?" "No."

The little house of Loreto had revealed to my heart something mysterious, and yet certain — a fourth way, of which the particulars were still unknown to me.

The Gospel Appeared to Be Completely New to Us

Q.: Four years later, the Focolare Movement was born. Could you briefly tell me how it began and how you started living its spirituality?

Chiara: The Movement started very simply in Trent, in the northern part of Italy, in 1943. The war was going on then and it was hitting our city too. I was living there with some of my friends. We were all very young and each one of us had an ideal as all young people do. One wanted to study, as was my case; one wanted to have a beautiful family; one wanted to build a nice home; one loved art. . . . But with the war and the bombings everything was crumbling, and we all realized that we could not reach the goals we had chosen for our lives. For instance, I couldn't continue with my studies; my friend's house was bombed; the one who wanted to get married couldn't do so because her fiancé was killed on the battlefront.

It seemed that these circumstances taught us a great lesson. They were preaching a terrific sermon: that "everything is vanity of vanities," that "everything passes." While all this was happening, together with this dramatic vision of things, an idea came which we think was an inspiration: Is there an ideal that won't pass, that no bomb can destroy? We understood that there was such an ideal. This ideal is God.

Therefore, God became everything in our lives. Naturally, even though we were very young, we were continuously facing death because the bomb shelters were not safe. At any moment we could leave this earth. This is why we had a great desire to find a way to live so that our lives would be in tune with our new-found ideal. One day, we were deeply impressed by a sentence of the New Testament: "Not he who says 'Lord, Lord'" – not he who calls or invokes God – "but he who does my will is the one who loves me." We understood that in order to have God as our ideal we had to do his will and not our will. We tried, moment by moment, to do not so much what we wanted, but rather what God was showing us through circumstances to be his will. At one point during these first days, we opened the Gospel and found another sentence that deeply struck us. It seemed to us to be — and it is — the synthesis of the Gospel, the last will that Jesus was leaving to mankind. "Love one another as I have loved you." This really impressed us. We looked at one another, this little group of girls, and we said, "Let's try to live it. I'll be ready to die for you and you have to be ready to die for her; we have to be ready to die for one another." And we started living this way.

The Lord was not always asking us to do heroic things for one another; at times he seemed to be asking smaller things from us: for example, to share our material possessions, to cry with those who were crying, to laugh with those who were laughing, to share the joys and the sufferings of others. In this way our lives really underwent a transformation, I would say a conversion.

The results were manifold. We experienced a fullness of joy, a great peace. But there was also something else. Since we read in the Scriptures, "Where charity and love abide, God abides," then in our effort to live this charity and love, we felt we experienced the presence of God in our midst. The God that we had chosen was now in the midst of us.

It was God, we think, who enlightened us and who made us understand a very important thing: the Gospel that we knew so well seemed to be completely new to us. Its words seemed startling. They were "words of life" and it was possible for everyone to live them. These words seemed to be unique, revolutionary, universal, made for everyone. We saw that in the Gospel there was the formula for the greatest revolution, the strongest revolution for all of mankind all over the world.

We started, therefore, to take these words one by one and to live them. They changed our relationship with God and with one another, not only in our little group, but also with all those whom we met. In short they created a Christian community around us. A scattered crowd made up of people who, although Christians, had ignored one another, became a unified group. After only a couple of months we were already five hundred, and among us one could see people, both young and old, with many different vocations. There were religious and laymen, children, mothers and fathers, all living the same ideal, that is, the will of God and the Gospel put into practice.

Every word of the Gospel seemed to open a new horizon before us, but some of them struck us in a special way. For example, "That all may be one," which indicated that our love had to be universal; or the phrase, "Where two or three are united in my name, I am there in the midst of them." Another one was, "Who listens to you, listens to me."

And I think that these three sentences were the guidelines of our Movement: that is, to open our hearts to all of humanity; to keep such a strong unity with one another as to have the presence of Christ in our midst; and to have such a strong unity with those who represented God on earth as to be a branch of the real vine which is the Church.

What happened, as a result of all this, was the presence

of God in our midst. It was He, therefore, who spread the Movement all over the world. In fact, we can now say that after thirty years of life, it has spread in such an extraordinary way that it cannot be attributed to any human person. For now we are on all the continents and in more than a hundred nations, and there are members of the Movement in all vocations.

One might ask, what are the fruits, what is it that is happening? The fruits are many and varied. For example, people convert to God, they find God. Atheism is overcome in many. There are sinners who come back with the desire of reaching sanctity, people who were confused and doubtful find the right path again. Another effect is the great number of vocations: people who understand more clearly that God is calling them, whether it be to the priesthood or to join a religious order or to form a beautiful family.

Furthermore, our Movement, even though it is a religious movement, is also laying down the basis for a new society. Its spirit brings new life to the world: it enlightens art and science, medicine and education, and all kinds of work.

We could ask ourselves now, what is so new about this vast Movement? In a certain sense, nothing is new because everything was already in the Gospel. What is new is the commitment of these people to live the Gospel. New also is the emphasis placed on particular truths which are quite relevant today, like unity, collective spirituality, living the communion of saints, all elements which characterize the spirituality of the Movement.

Also new, perhaps, is the way of conveying these truths, that is, not so much through words but through life. Especially new, I think, is the love, this current, this invasion of love, that the Movement is bringing about, and we all know that love makes all things new.

The Secret of Our Commitment

Q.:   The most striking thing in the Focolare Movement is the collective commitment that animates it. What is the secret behind it?

Chiara: It is not a collective commitment that we make in order to be part of this Movement. It is a personal commitment that each one makes.

The choice of God, as I said before, demands something which sounds almost like a paradox in our society, but still is extremely valid: the choice of suffering, the choice of the cross. The words of Christ, "Whoever wants to be my disciple must deny himself, take up his cross, and follow me," are also for our times. This is the choice that every person in the Movement makes. Our personal sufferings, darkness, loneliness, the awareness of our limitations, etc., instead of being obstacles, are almost springboards to carry us further ahead. Why? Because the cross is not only not put aside, but is loved and embraced; at times even sought. We try to recognize it not only in ourselves, but also in others, in all those who suffer, in individuals as well as in those parts of the Mystical Body of Christ where the Church is in greatest difficulty. We also recognize the cross in the various social environments where suffering is more evident; for example, in the developing countries where hunger is widespread and freedom is threatened.

Therefore, the fundamental reality that we must anchor ourselves to is the cross.

Q.: The basis for such a great development of the Movement is therefore this love for the cross. Could you tell us more about it?

Chiara: Certainly. Since the beginning, in all circumstances, we tried to love the cross as much as we could. Knowing that we had but one life to live, we were anxious to understand what Jesus' greatest suffering was. You know how generous young people are, and I think we were too: thus we wanted to give our life to Jesus, to follow him crucified and in his greatest suffering. We had heard from a priest that his greatest suffering was when he cried: "My God, my God, why have you forsaken me?" That is, when on the cross he felt himself rejected by earth and, in a certain sense, by heaven as well. Heaven was closed for him. We said, "Since we have only one life, we want to live it for him, we want to search for him." For this reason, we find him in our personal sufferings, in that darkness that we spoke about before, that solitude, that sense of being orphans that we feel at times. This is so because he is the orphan in the highest sense of the word, the one who was most alone, the one who suffered the greatest darkness.

Thus, we meet him also in all those who suffer, like the sick, the orphan, and the sinner because they remind us of Jesus Forsaken, who took upon himself man's sins. He wasn't a sinner, of course, but he made himself "sin" for us. He made himself "excommunication" for us, "separation" for us, "atheism" for us. Therefore, all of these are for us the figure of Jesus Forsaken. They attract us. We feel that we are in the world in order to embrace all its loneliness and abandonment—inasmuch as we are capable of doing so—having before us the figure of him forsaken and his cry, "My God, my God, why have you forsaken me?"

The "Fourth Way"

Q.: If you don't mind, I'd like to go back to your first answer, when you mentioned that first intuition you had in Loreto regarding the 'fourth way" of which the particulars were still unknown to you. Has this become a reality in the Movement? How?

Chiara: Yes, it has become a reality in the Focolare. The Focolare is the fundamental unit of our movement and was the first to be born. It represents a novelty in the Church and it was especially a novelty thirty years ago.

In those days, in fact, a young woman had only three possible choices: marriage, the convent, or consecration to God while remaining in one's own home.

The Focolare, then, appeared from its beginning as a

Above: **Loreto, Italy,** where Chiara Lubich attended a convention in 1939. Inside the basilica, there is said to be the house in which the Holy Family dwelled. Chiara relates how "The little house of Loreto had revealed to my heart something mysterious, and yet certain — a fourth way, of which the particulars were still unknown to me."
Below: **2 Cappuccini Square** was the home of the first Focolare. Today there are Focolare Centers in twenty-nine nations in every continent.

Above: **Men's Focolare** in Brooklyn, New York.

Below: **Women's Focolare** in Astoria, New York.

"fourth way." It met all the aspirations of those girls, and later on of the young men, who were called to be part of it. They, in fact, felt the vocation to follow the Gospel with all its demands: to leave "father, mother, brothers, sisters and fields" in order to follow Jesus, which was not possible in marriage, nor in the life of people consecrated to God while remaining at home. They wanted the atmosphere of a supernatural family, which would go over and above the relationships existing in a natural family. This was not always found in convents. They wanted a total consecration to God and this as well did not exist in a natural family.

The only possible model for this new kind of calling was the family of Nazareth. The family atmosphere certainly wasn't missing there, and at the same time, it was a family made up of people who were all virgins. They were living together in order to fulfill God's plans, leaving everything behind them. The family of Nazareth appeared to be like all other families. The Focolarini, too, wanted to appear as small groups of people who live together as a normal family.

The Focolare, in time, developed its rule of life. In order to maintain its characteristic of being a real supernatural family, we wanted to give first priority to that mutual and continual charity which guarantees the presence of Jesus among the members of the Movement. This norm, now approved by the Church, has to be considered before any other norm.

Jesus among two or more: this is and must be the Focolare. Focolare, therefore, is a presence of Christ in the world.

There are now more than two hundred Focolare centers all over the world. The whole Movement in all its variety revolves around them as if around the jewels of a watch.

Therefore, the Focolare is light and salt. It is made up of members of the most varied social classes, nationalities and races, bearing witness to the universality of the Movement.

There is another element which makes the Focolare something new. It is not made up only of people who choose to live a celibate life, but it also includes married people who share the same life, with equal rights and duties. They feel the calling to be totally of God, spiritually, even though their participation in the life of the Focolare is obviously limited by their family duties. They live in their own homes.

This was made possible by the fact that the ideal of the Focolare, as of the whole Movement, is supernatural love — charity — which is possible for all.

As the years passed by, we saw that it was possible for the married Focolarini to make promises, just as the Focolarini living in community take vows. Their promises are those of poverty, chastity and obedience lived according to their state of life and the teachings of the Church.

Other norms are followed by the members of a Focolare, but they are all concrete expressions of love: for instance, putting all possessions in common; spreading in the world the ideal that animates the Focolare; preserving its deep spirituality and the spiritual path of each member and sustaining it by the prayer life which the Church suggests for the faithful; caring for one's health; providing the clothing and the home which, because of charity, must always be in harmony with one's environment; studying religious subjects to supplement the wisdom which the Holy Spirit pours abundantly into hearts united in charity; undertaking professional studies so that the Christian character will be rooted in a person who is as perfect as possible; and, finally, circulating new information, using all the available media to keep the Focolare all over the world constantly informed about what is happening. In this way, we can always be one heart and one mind, sharing all together the joys and the sufferings that accompany the development of such a vast movement.

These norms came from life. Nothing had been foreseen, since nobody ever decided to found a Focolare. It happened through circumstances. We must say, therefore, that it was really the love of Jesus that did everything.

Q.: Many say that the characteristic of the Focolarini is joy. And one can see it. What is the formula?

Chiara: We spoke about the cross as a means to love God. Well, in an extraordinary way, we experienced the fact that joy is the effect of this life, of this choice.

Joy is the very fruit of love. Joy is the atmosphere of the Christian community. Joy is the characteristic of committed Christians. In fact, Jesus, before dying (and we know how he died), promised his disciples the fullness of joy.

2. THIRTY YEARS OF THE FOCOLARE MOVEMENT

After my dialogue with the foundress of the Movement, I began meeting other persons who are specially committed to the various activities of the Focolare Movement. The following is an interview with Guglielmo Boselli, an architect and editor of Città Nuova *the Italian edition of the magazine* Living City, *which is one of the publications of the Movement.*

The Same Discovery Today as in the Beginning

Q.: I would like to reminisce just this once, Guglielmo, about the early days of the Focolare Movement. I remember how deeply struck I was in meeting the first group of young men and women who had found, as they said, the "Ideal." Perhaps you were among them. I was deeply moved as they spoke to me, their eyes shining with joy, about a revolution of love that would set the world on fire. It seemed as though leading men to unity through charity would take a matter of days. Thirty years have passed and the Movement is now all over the world. How would you evaluate the growth and success of the Movement in light of the hopes and expectations you had at the beginning?

Guglielmo: Before starting, we have to make a distinc-

tion, a very clear distinction between the inspiration that
gave birth to and sustained the Movement throughout the
years, and the people who, with their faults, weaknesses,
and failures to respond to the gift given to them, are a part
of it. I am answering your questions to say what I think
the Lord has done, not what we do or often undo. If it
were not for this reason, I wouldn't open my mouth. The
work done by God, however, should be recognized and not
belittled. Almost in spite of us, God has done and is doing
great things.

A few days ago, I attended a meeting for a large group
of Gen* boys and girls. I found in them the same
overwhelming enthusiasm which I felt when I first met the
"Ideal" twenty-four years ago. It was a powerful experience, almost unbelievable, for it seemed as though none of
the turmoil (confrontations, protests, ideological struggles,
cultural revolutions, rebellion in schools, and so on) which
had swept over the world during these past years, had ever
happened. Yet, I could sense in this large gathering that the
young people had become more sensitive to the problems
of the world and more aware of them because of the events
I have mentioned. But something much stronger and far
more fascinating had taken them, just as we had been taken
a long time ago. In spite of the changed circumstances, it
was the same divine attraction, the same discovery of God
in our midst, of the presence of Christ among us. It was a

*See Chapter "Gen: The Second Generation."

discovery of how full the interior life can be, an unquestioned certainty that in Him everything is possible. When I was listening to them, everything around us seemed to be fake, as if it would be enough to blow hard to make everything crumble. We must realize, however, that this overpowering change in our lives surely does not come from flesh and blood, but from the Spirit which is given by God to those who accept it. It is like an initial grace, and, little by little, one has to learn how to put it into practice, just as small children, who are first held in their mother's arms, must learn how to walk by themselves. When a person, or a movement, begins to walk alone, there are steps to be climbed, hurdles to be overcome. It's a whole life to be lived. Growth brings about a greater depth, prepares us for an inner asceticism, leads us closer to the moment of the cross, to experiences which Jesus had experienced.

At the beginning, He shows us, in the fullness of light, the total gift of Himself, calling us to repeat it in our life. Then, we have to walk a long way with Him in order to reach that point of self-donation. In this way, the initial enthusiasm and thrust become substance, a reality of life, through difficulties, defeats, moments of light, misunderstandings, mistakes due to lack of experience, etc., and it ultimately produces the solid results you call the success of the Movement that one can see today. I believe it is because some or many have gone through this experience that the other day I could sense in those young people the same drive we had at the beginning. Some "build," at times

Fr. Pascal Foresi, the first Focolarino to become a priest, has contributed to the birth and development of the Focolare by working in close cooperation with Chiara Lubich as the Ecclesiastical Assistant to the Movement.

Fontem, West Cameroon. A Focolarina who is part of the team of doctors, nurses, teachers, and technicians who have brought about the birth of the town of Fontem. In the picture she is shown with one of the chiefs of the Bangwa tribe of the Fontem Valley during a celebration.

through great suffering or by going ahead blindly, but the result is that the fruit is as genuine as the plant which grew it. For me, this is the greatest miracle that God works in His Works when they are truly His and rooted in the Gospel. It has to be the Gospel as it is, however, not watered down with a lot of reasoning or personal and partial viewpoints.

You asked me how I would evaluate the Movement's development in these last thirty years as compared to our early expectations. It would be like comparing a grown-up person to a newborn baby. You cannot make a comparison, and yet they are the same person with the same features; the same person, therefore, with all the maturity acquired through the years.

I have to add one more thing. Thirty years ago, we were few, almost exclusively Italians, with a still very limited experience. What is extraordinary today is that this same life has spread with similar thrust among Chinese, Chileans, Brazilians, North Americans, Australians, Africans, Germans, French, English, and so on. Furthermore, it has gone beyond the Catholic world. Anglicans and Lutherans have made it their own, as have Moslems, Buddhists, and others.

It is quite probable that the early Christians too had the impression that the Kingdom of God would spread very quickly. We know, however, that it took centuries of persecutions, martyrdoms, difficulties of all kinds before it actually spread all over the world which was known at that time. I think that what we are living, in our limited proportion, of course, is an experience of this kind.

An Even Stronger Commitment

Q.: The Focolare Movement, it seems to me, was the first movement aiming at the primacy of charity. Then the Second Vatican Council took place; it put the primacy of charity at the foundation of the Church's renewal. From the expressions used by most people and the ideas I hear about, it seems that the message of the Focolarini has been picked up throughout the entire Catholic Church. Do you think the Movement has completed its task?

Guglielmo: Not at all. Just the opposite is true. In fact, to give charity the first place has become a common effort, at least, as you say, "in the expression." If this tendency, however, doesn't find the way to become a living reality, everything can become empty knowledge. Unless we focus on the true meaning of the word charity, we may end up, as has already happened in other eras, just identifying it with some external aspects of it. In the past, at times, it meant only works of mercy; now it could become just social involvement, or if you want, a revolutionary political commitment, and so on. This is the danger we are facing today, that tends involuntarily to deprive the Christian revolution of its deepest content. Charity, of course, consists also of the things we have mentioned; but before everything else, it is important to bring the real meaning of charity into focus within and among men, because it is the substance of everything else. Without it our actions become just pious works, unionism, socialism, or paternalism, according to the circumstances. There would be many things to say about this. God seems to send His charisms where He wants. And in our movement He has given a charism to put into life the unity spoken of by the Council. I am not saying that He has given it only to the Focolare, but that He certainly gave us a gift which is not only for the Movement, but for the Church, and for all mankind.

In the midst of many social and political tensions dominating our world, we must remember that the Christian revolution does not stem from politics or from economic and social actions (although we have to do our part to remedy many situations), but from the rediscovery of Christ. It is Christ who changes the world. The young people have already realized this in many places, and it is from them that the answers for tomorrow shall come.

The great novelty which has turned the old spiritual patterns upside down is the discovery not only of the Christ in our intimate personal life, but of the "collective Christ." In other words, the novelty is a collective spirituality, the "building" of Christ within the community. It is a new kind of asceticism, in a way, able to fulfill the desire for unity felt by many.

If, on the one hand, the Council has created in the whole Church a new awareness of collective reality, on the other hand, it has also placed before those who have chosen this reality as their ideal in life, a greater responsibility to their commitment. If we had previously felt that we had to bear witness to our Christianity from an avant-garde position, now we feel that our efforts must be doubled.

Yes, we often speak of charity, but what can be done to make it become a real way of living? How can we make it the normal way of acting in the local community, in the family, at work, or at school? How can we bring this charity into general norms of behavior in order for it to penetrate social and political structures, as well as the fields of art and education, and the relationships between races and nations?

Do you think that with these challenges before it the Movement has exhausted its task? I would say that, on the contrary, we have only just begun. It is the Council itself which asks us to bring our contribution everywhere, together with all Christians of good will. We are not talking about a clamorous, noisy contribution, but a positive, silent way of service. It is for this reason that the Movement is called "The Work of Mary." In the early Church, Mary was not an authority or a law-giver, yet her presence had a definite influence on the life of the early Christian community. We would like to imitate her, as much as possible, in the heart of the Church. We would like to be as she was, a presence, a vital reality which changes things from within.

I'll give you a good example of what I mean. On visiting the little town of Fontem in Cameroon, an African bishop said, "It seemed to me that there was the beginning of something of the New Jerusalem." Why? Because the charism, that "key" to open the doors to unity, worked in Fontem. And I do not speak of a unity of action, or of work, or of plans, but a unity in Christ, which rendered the early Christian communities new, and which

Manila, Philippines. *Above:* A carpentry shop where many young men learn a trade.

Right: This family is one among many others which have been able to leave the miserable slums of "Tondo." It has found a temporary home in one of the houses provided by the communion of goods among the people of the Movement, while helping them to find the way to support themselves.

Recife, Brazil: Medical aid in the slums of Recife in the North-East of Brazil. Here the Movement has set up an intense social action program.

changes the world because it allows Christ to work, instead of us wanting to do everything in His place. Christianity didn't come to Fontem mixed with the white, Western mentality. It came as a presence: without a lot of clamor, but truly real; without words, but with facts and through life . . . a transparent Gospel that has no nation or race and is made for all. In Fontem it has been accepted by all. It hasn't abolished the local civilization, but has enhanced all that was positive in it. According to many African leaders, this is what Africa needs today.

The little town of Fontem is one of the first tangible results, but it shows how much still needs to be done. From many parts of Africa, from Zaire to the Ivory Coast, to Uganda, they are asking for Focolare Centers. Many African missionary priests and sisters go to Fontem for training in living out their commitment. As I said, this is the beginning, ninety-nine per cent still needs to be done.

Of course, I don't want to give you the impression I am boasting about the Movement. As I mentioned at the beginning of this interview, we are what we are, and Jesus didn't say, "Where two saints are united in my name. . . ." He simply said, "Where two or three are united in my name, I am there in their midst."

The Ideal and the Structure from a Single Inspiration

Q.: The ideal of unity in charity, "that all may be one," which inspires the Focolare Movement, is undoubtedly a universal ideal going beyond all borders, recognizing no barriers. Don't you think, however, that there is a contradiction between this universal ideal which the Movement proclaims and the internal structures of the Movement, which define it? Isn't there the danger that placing it next to other religious institutions practically limits its boundaries and identifies it as a particular segment of the whole.

Guglielmo: There is no doubt that we are a segment, a detail of the whole. The Movement has been given a charism, and in the Church there are, have been, and always will be, innumerable charisms. Denying this would mean to doubt the Holy Spirit's creativity. Our task is to bring our charism, and place it side by side with the others, in a spirit of love which is not closed in but universal and open to all. The proof of this is that the Movement is accepted by Moslems, Buddhists, and even atheists who regard the Movement with interest and with hope.

Now to answer your question about our internal structures. Christ Himself, for that matter, was incarnate, became a particular man, and never left Palestine. When He founded the Church, in order to accomplish unity among all men, He established a particular structure made up of twelve apostles among whom he chose Peter; then there were the seventy-two disciples, and so on. A spirituality without a structure is like the wind. It is not a human reality. One is not made of soul alone. It would not make sense. There must be a defined body to house the spirit. The same is true for the Church and for the vital experiences born and developed throughout the Church's history.

The beauty of the Church is that she is always alive and furnishing experiences that are not closed in on themselves, but offered as gifts, services, proposals to all and for all.

As for us, I have already told you that the Movement wanted to be called "The Work of Mary." We have often made of Mary a distorted cliché, a little statue, or a series of special devotions. Mary is something else. First of all, she is the layperson par excellence! Secondly, she is the prototype of the Christian, the model that everyone can follow. Christ is the Son of God; Mary is only a creature. This is why she is the attainable model for all. She is the way to live Christ. Furthermore, she is the one who gave birth to Christ: she is the mother of God and of the Church.

These are not merely nice thoughts; it is the truth and the truth has a decisive impact on the history of mankind, as well as of the Church. Mary gave birth to Christ. She teaches us the way to "give birth" to Christ in the world and also within the Christian community, so that He may live again in today's society.

Mary was not the entire early Church. She was one among many. She brought, however, a universal reality, and in her there were, somehow, all the vocations. There was also all of the future Church. This then is what we feel we must imitate. We must be a Movement among many others in the Church and relive Mary. We know we are not the only ones doing this, but we feel we are called to do it. This makes our calling at one and the same time universal and particular.

If you look at how the Movement came about (and it was not through abstract reasonings, but always as a result of life), you can see that around the first nucleus of Focolarine with Chiara Lubich, our foundress, a community flourished. Since the beginning, it was made up of persons from different vocations, characteristics, ages, classes, cultures, and so on. In the heart of this community, some young people spontaneously felt the desire to make a total commitment of themselves in order to be instruments in the fulfillment of the "that all may be one" ideal that you mentioned. Later on, there were also priests and religious who also wanted to pattern their lives according to this spirit of unity, giving a new vigor to their particular vocation. Many laypeople, in the meantime, chose to commit themselves to bringing this new spirit into the social context of their lives. The present structures of the Movement matured with this vital growth: actually all the vocations and realities of the Church are present in them. There are the Focolarini, who have vows and live in common; the married Focolarini; the "Volunteers"; the priests' branch; the religious, both men and women; the New Family Movement; the New Parish Movement; the Movement for a New Humanity; and the Gen Movement.

Someone has stated that "the 'Work of Mary' is a movement in the Church, and therefore a part of the Church. But it is just as true that, in its deepest reality, it is the whole Church living in a particular community."

It seems to us that this is God's plan for the Movement. Then, we are what we are, perhaps erring, or slowing down

The Blue Sisters founded by Chiara Lubich. They are Focolarine-sisters. They receive their training in the spirituality together with the other Focolarine. The Blue Sisters emphasize the aspect of the religious life, while the Focolarine consider themselves lay persons consecrated to God.

The Focolare publishes twelve magazines in nine languages.

God's action all the time, or diminishing what His wisdom had given to us. We can also fall into the temptation of being closed in on ourselves. These are the risks present in every human reality. But we cannot deny that God is working in a way which is far superior and out of proportion to what we are doing. In order to experience this, it would be enough to participate in any one of the summer Mariapolises where this "testimony of the Church" is expressed.

What I am trying to point out, because I have often experienced it, is that a dualism between the spirit and the structure cannot exist in the works of God. The same inspiration caused Jesus to say, "blessed are the poor. . ." and "love one another as I have loved you," and also to build His Church in a certain way. And so it is with the works of God. The structures are not something outside of, or in opposition to, the spirituality which inspires them. They are not precluded from, or limited by, the spirit; on the contrary, the structures are the instruments best suited for spreading the spirit. Of course, those who make up these structures can also ruin everything by their foolishness. But this depends on us and not on the structures themselves. And it is also clear that the structures will be dynamically adapted to the times.

The Meaning of Our Obedience

Q.: I have never met anybody, either for or against the Focolare Movement, who would not acknowledge the Movement's unfailing obedience to the Church. According to some, the Focolarini are today the only heirs of that distinctive sign that once made others obedient to the Pope "unto death." This attitude of total obedience, with that absolute availability it entails, presupposes a concept of authority which, to say the least, is outmoded today. In fact, some people seem to think more and more that obedience is no longer a virtue. What do you think?

Guglielmo: Of course, there is obedience and obedience. There is fearful, subservient, and exterior obedience, and then there is the conscious, adult obedience of those who want to be active, constructive members of the Church. These latter ones believe that they are the Church and that there exists not only the charism for the specific, local Christian communities, but also the charism of guidance and of teaching that belongs to the successors of the apostles. In other words, they consider the institutional Church not only as a human reality with defects which are characteristic of human realities, but also as a divine reality. They love the Church and live to enhance its unity, considering all divisions as obstacles to the development of God's kingdom. However, they are aware of the fact that in the context of unity, there can be a legitimate pluralism in theological research and vital experiences.

Some attention should be given to those who with good

will are trying to bring forward a deepening, in an evangelical sense, of the life of the Church. We are among these. That which we think to be one of the obstacles to unity (the reason for which Christ let himself be nailed to the cross) is a certain spirit of bitter complaint, a certain poison of inner hostility which can exist at times, despite the best of intentions.

As far as authority is concerned, we have to distinguish between authority and authoritarianism. Authoritarianism must be overcome, but not authority, when it is clearly understood.

Also in the matter of obedience, we have chosen Jesus as our model and he was obedient unto death. It is certainly difficult at times to give up even our inspirations. However, we feel that this is the very sign of their authenticity. And it is the way that all the saints throughout history have followed. They were willing to bow their heads before the authority of the Church.

Since the beginning of the Movement, it has always been very clear to us that the Gospel had to be lived in its entirety without leaving aside even one of the words of life contained therein. Otherwise, it would be like leaving aside a part of Christ. In the Gospel we find Jesus gave the apostles, who were the first bishops, these words of life: "he who listens to you, listens to me." We have always taken these words as a rule of life.

I can assure you that, looking at things from outside the logic of the Gospel, we have been in circumstances when it was difficult to put these words into practice. It cost us a lot to do it, but we never doubted them, not even in the darkest moments when the very basis of the ideal we were starting to live seemed to be destroyed. We never doubted that the Church is guided by God and that she is our mother, even when she guides and corrects. And the result of this adherence has been that not a thread, not even the boldest ideas of the initial inspiration of the Movement, were not accepted by the Church. She showed herself to be a real mother. . . and this was even before the Vatican Council took place.

We do not want to judge those who think differently about obedience than we do. However, we see obedience as Pope John did — to use a well-known example. He made obedience the plan of his life. In fact, his motto was "obedientia et pax" (obedience and peace). Can you tell me if there was ever another man in the Church who was freer than he? He possessed that freedom which comes when, completely losing ourselves, we leave room only for Christ in us.

It is certainly true that in the history of the Church there have been, are, and will probably always be bishops and others who are fearful of what is new. They might be closed and authoritarian, but just the same, it is true that the "obedient man sings victory."

If a work is from God, then the Holy Spirit enlightens those who are in positions of authority. Perhaps, through corrections, or criticisms, or limitations, God purifies His work and makes it more His own. This has been our experience.

When obedience is not passive acquiescence, but active, conscious participation dictated by a profound "sense of the Church," then we see that today, as always, obedience is a fundamental virtue. It is also true that if I love my mother, I naturally do what she asks of me. It doesn't make sense that, if I want to achieve unity among all, I would start by eliminating those very people who represent the pillars chosen by Jesus to guarantee the unity of the body of the Church.

We are convinced that beyond all passing fads, this firmness in remaining attached to the "rock" is one of the Movement's strongest assets. Many things will come and go in the Church, but in the end, certain basic pillars which today are being questioned, and among these is obedience, will be able to withstand the storms.

However, we too have our own way of protesting against authoritarianism. When those people who hold positions of responsibility meet the Movement, they rediscover the true meaning of authority as service. Its spirit helps them to listen to all, to value the participation of everyone, to sincerely want only what God wants, and to make decisions, whenever possible, expressions of unity and not impositions. And, at the same time, we ask the others to love those who are in authority, and to consider them as the first brothers to be loved; we ask them not to place themselves in opposition to authority, but rather to be open and ready to do whatever is asked; we even ask them to believe that those who are in authority have the grace to understand the problems and that the solution will be more enlightened the more they are an expression of the charity that is lived by all. This will happen when each one will lose his own point of view in order to want only what God would want in his place. In this way, relationships will change profoundly and everyone will be completely free and completely one.

Responding to Vatican II

Q.: It is generally believed that, after the wave of renewal brought on by the Council, there is a mounting tide in favor of a return to previous ways. There is much denouncing of the brakes being applied, of steps being taken backwards, and even of the Council being betrayed. It is an everyday topic from which much of today's Catholic protest draws its ammunition. There are voices that are missing in this chorus of protest, the voices of the Focolarini. They should be the first to react to every attack on the Council that had so fully endorsed their message. Why this silence? Aren't you afraid that the silence might indirectly play into the hands of those who are trying to do away with the work of the Council?

Guglielmo: This question is in a way bound to the preceding one. I will answer it with a thought expressed in the magazine *Concilium,* published by a group of well-known European theologians in order to continue the work of the Council. In a recent analysis of the various movements of spiritual awakening, the *Concilium* states that the most successful ones are those in harmony with the Ecclesiastical authorities, because they see this commitment of unity to the Church as one of the means and one of the goals of the awakening itself. The Focolare Movement is the first one mentioned on the list of all these movements.

We are convinced that the best way to preserve what the Council brought about and the most vigorous way to fulfill its plan is to put its teachings into practice. We should live what the Council said, apply its instructions with enthusiasm, and concentrate our efforts primarily on its main line of conduct, which is a spiritual renewal from within and the primacy of charity. This is all too often forgotten, perhaps because it is the most difficult and demanding part, and yet everything else depends on and gains its meaning from this. Above all, this is what we are trying to do. In fact, I would say that this is the reason for the Movement's existence.

In this regard, there is something we note happening every day, and that is, that when we are able to give the Gospel in its genuine form lived to the fullest, we see that both conservatives and progressives, as if by some miracle, agree. They discover something that goes beyond the level of their debates or that which gives rise to their differences. It is that something which is really *new* and which we think should be put in full sight for all to see. Otherwise the Council itself, instead of becoming the reason for a greater maturity and unity, could degenerate into quarrels between the more or less progressive and the more or less conservative factions.

It will be life which will have the final victory and which will succeed in changing what has to be changed. We have experienced many times that, when faced with the reality of life, the barriers that should come down will crumble. Many prejudices and narrow-minded ideas fall away, and what comes into relief and remains standing is what is authentic. Here, too, we have to believe that, in the end, it is Christ who changes the world. When we with our lives give proof of his presence among Christians, then He, who is Light, clarifies, transforms, and renews the Church.

All this must be done silently, in humility, with patience and charity. There are also other bold and vital works in the Church, such as the Little Brothers and the Little Sisters of Foucauld and others, which are also building on solid foundations. A recent article in a leading European newspaper mentions that these are the most consistent and solid religious movements of our day.

I could cite many other instances of the contribution we are trying to make in this way, the contribution on which everything else depends.

It is justly said today that Christians have a duty to face the problems of the Third World, poverty, etc. There is, however, a direct way of getting involved, of personally sharing the lot of the most miserable and of building something together with them. There are certain situations like the famous Tondo, a shantytown near Manila, where, with dignity, Volunteers of the Movement are rebuilding a "society," sharing whatever they have, perhaps their poverty, their suffering, their life placed at the service of the others, and in this way they are taking steps forward, out of the humiliating situation in which the rest of society has placed them. Or else, there are the inhabitants of the "Mocambos" (slums) on the island of Santa Teresinha in Recife who, through a similar experience, are able to bring themselves up from their misery because someone is working with them, side by side, without trying to change them or make them something they are not. Instead, they simply propose to live together according to the law of the Gospel. Of course, this does not exclude the fact that the Movement is likewise committed to changing oppressive social structures.

Another thing is that many priests today are suffering from an identity crisis. Very often they feel isolated and estranged; they are not able to find a true rapport with people or to build around them the Christian community. There are some who even lose their sense of vocation. But then you should see those parishes where priests of the Movement have begun to live (first among themselves, and then with others,) the simple and pure experience of the Gospel. You can see the desert blossoming again around them. Certainly, they were not leaning on old schemes; they started from zero. And what at first seemed impossible is now accomplished. These are very lively communities which have become centers of interest for others. They have become a penetrating force of Christianity in a de-christianized world.

I could continue mentioning similar experiences about

what the Movement has done in the family, in education, and in many kinds of work. Believe me, there is a silence that is more vocal than many words. It is the silence of those who try to bring new life. It is an explosive silence.

The Coordinating Council. All the Branches (Focolarini, Volunteers, Priests, Religious, Gen), and the Mass Movements (New Families, New Humanity Movement, Priests' Movement, New Parishes, and Youth Movement) are represented in the General Coordinating Council of the Focolare Movement in Rome, Italy.

Genfest 1975, Rome, Italy. On March 1st, 1975, 25,000 young people crowd the sports arena in Rome for the music festival sponsored by the Gen Movement. Through their songs, panto-mimes, dances, and sharing of experiences, the Gen show the vitality of their Ideal: God. Genfests also take place in many other cities all over the world attracting crowds of young people.

3. GEN: THE SECOND GENERATION

Twenty-five years after its beginning, the Focolare Movement has seen the birth of its second generation. "Gen," in fact, stands for "New Generation." The following is an interview with Silvana Veronesi and Peppuccio Zanghi, who are responsible for the World Gen Centers near Rome.

A Different Logic

Q.: Today's youth are at the center of a world that assails them from all sides. Each side is trying to win them over, to lure them in all kinds of ways and with all kinds of attractions — from drugs and sex, to violence, to revolutionary ideas, to militancy, to success and money. The Gen Movement, however, offers only one thing, the Gospel, and not an easy watered-down Gospel at that. It is a Gospel that is to be lived completely, in its entirety and fullness. Yet, many young people respond. I must admit that I have some difficulty fitting this picture into the reality of our present-day world. Could you help me by shedding some light on this phenomenon?

Silvana: I don't think we can compare the attractions of society, including all the things you have just mentioned, to what a movement like the Gen has to offer to the young people of today. It is an entirely different picture because the Gen Movement is part of a work of God. It is the second generation of the Focolare Movement and, therefore, it clearly belongs on a spiritual plane.

That's why the Gen Movement, (as you know, the name stands for "New Generation") was not afraid from the very beginning to propose to the youth a goal that I would call heroic, because the model and the ideal it chose was not just Jesus, but Jesus Crucified. One would think that such a proposal would frighten the young people away. Actually because of its truthfulness and openess, it is the only proposal that attracts the young people to make a.choice. Those who have said "yes" are truly and seriously committed.

Peppuccio: It is true; God has His own way of seeing and answering men's problems. God's logic is different from ours. We have seen from experience that it is not true that young people cannot understand it. Of course, they have to take a big step, but the young do not refuse to do it. On the contrary, it is what they are waiting for. And God answers on another level. His answer is not a theory, but a person who has a name, the name Jesus. I saw, for example, that if you speak to young people about abstract ideals of perfection, of virtue or of purity, they do not understand. But, if you show them a person who was like this, who really lived like this, then they understand. This person is Jesus. The answer of God, the logic of God, is Jesus. Take, for instance, the relationship between boys and girls. If you try to tackle this problem merely on the level of human psychology, or sociology, and so on, you realize that for every answer there is another side of the matter. But if you tell them, it is Jesus who proposes that you behave like this because He himself lived like this, then you will find that the young not only accept it but are also able to make others understand their behavior. Actually, if you look at the Gospel you will see that it contains the answer to all the aspirations of young people today. The Gospel taken in its entirety is revolution; it is authenticity; it is poverty. So, if the Gen want to go against the current, if they actually love going against the current, it is because they are in love with their leader, Jesus, who went against the current in the highest sense.

Silvana: In synthesis, this going against the current means "to give." It is this giving without any selfish limitations, this giving all, that answers the young people's need to completely fulfill themselves. They find the answer in giving rather than in having or receiving.

Peppuccio: And it is not so much a giving of what we have but of what we are. The young people feel this very strongly. This "giving," in fact, was the basis for the birth of the Gen Movement.

A Structure That Is Charity

Q.: Every so often I hear news of big Gen meetings, encounters, congresses, get-togethers; and while I am happy about it, I must admit that I have always felt a healthy skepticism in regard to mass manifestations. It is a skepticism that grows in relation to the vast proportions of these manifestations. At best, they can measure the enthusiasm of a particular moment. But then, I cannot help asking myself what will remain of all that enthusiasm, those commitments and resolutions of the moment, when the young people return to their everyday lives between one meeting and the next. Perhaps only a little remains! I would like you to show me that my skepticism is out of place as far as the Gen Movement is concerned.

Silvana: Well, to this we must explain, first of all, how the Gen Movement is comprised. It is a very large movement made up of young people from all countries of the world, actually from all five continents. Thus they are very different in culture, in background and in age — from the smallest whom we call Gen 4; to the eight to thirteen-year-old group, the Gen 3; to high school and university students, the Gen 2. They belong to different social classes, customs, and even religions. There are, in fact, many non-Catholic and even non-Christian Gen.

At the heart of the movement there is a core group, since the Gen Movement is evangelical. What did Jesus do? He chose some who were closest to him, the twelve apostles. Then there were all the others who followed him; those for whom he multiplied the loaves of bread, for whom he performed miracles, who listened fascinated by his words. But it was the twelve apostles whom he relied on to carry out his work in the midst of these masses. It's the same in the Gen Movement, where this core group of

Above: **The "Gen Fuoco" from Florence, Italy,** one of the many Gen musical groups, expresses through modern musical forms the new life experienced in living the Gospel.

Below: **A group of girls performs a pantomime.** Pantomimes have proven to be one of the most effective forms of art used by the Gen to communicate their message.

A panoramic view of the sports arena in Vicenze, Italy, where 4,000 young people are gathered for a Youth-Day.

Berlin, Germany. 3,000 young people take part in the Genfest in the Berlin *Sporthalle.* The Genfest is a new kind of celebration: through their performances the Gen express the desire to answer basic questions: why live under stress? Why exploitation? What is the meaning of life?

those who wish to be fully committed represent the backbone, the skeleton, as it were. However, it is also true that not all remain committed to the end. Even among the twelve chosen by Jesus there was one who defected.

And what about the others in the Gen Movement? They are all influenced to a certain degree. All that is asked of them is to live the Gospel, pure and simple, without any added structures. Yet, it is certain that something new will come because of it, as happens at times when we see a human or social desire which can only be explained as a result of the influence of the seed of Christianity that had been deposited in mankind long before.

Q.: But the more committed Gen, those whom you call the backbone or skeleton of the Movement, do they have a structure of their own?

Peppuccio: Yes, they do, but it is a special structure. It is nothing else but charity entering and govering all the different aspects of their lives. Of course there are consequences. The Gen have a very intense and continuous desire for unity among themselves. They want a total sharing not only of what they have but of what they are. The mature Gen put everything in common; they share experiences of their lives, they share their money (and not just what is extra but every penny they have), their talents, and their time. None of this has ever been asked of or imposed upon them. It blossomed from the spirit of the movement and was created by the Gen themselves who live it with true unanimity of thought.

Leaving The Old Patterns Behind

Q.: The problems which most interest young people today are the social ones. So, I would like to know how the young people in the Gen Movement are able to translate their spiritual ideal into a concrete Christian testimony that has a practical impact on Society?

Peppuccio: The young people are deeply convinced that today we are living in an important period of transition from a series of separate cultures (European, South American, Chinese, and so on) to a unified planetary culture. Since they feel very strongly about this, they have coined a phrase for it. They say, we are now going from the European man, the African, the Australian, etc., to the "world man." That's why, on the social plane, they want to work on a world basis. And because they would like this universal commitment to be the fruit of new psychological structures, they want to be men, and Christians, before being American, French, German, Italian, African, and so on. And this is also the way, although it may seem apparently longer, toward building social structures that are truly new, leaving behind old nationalistic, racial, and other discriminatory patterns.

This brings about completely different ways of thinking and of speaking, for it leads to the discovery that certain ways of facing the social problems of the world suffer from narrowness, because we continue looking at these problems according to a particular mentality, for instance, with a strictly Western mentality.

New York City, April 27, 1976. During a Youth Day. *Above:*
Some of the Gen who have shared their experiences. *Below:*
The audience participates in the singing.

Above: **Brazilian Gen from Sao Paulo** making plans for a project of social work. *Below:* **World Gen Center in Rome.** Some of the girls representing different continents.

Obviously, this commitment has to be made concrete and, therefore, the Gen have begun, at least for now, by focusing on one continent. They chose Africa because here the Western world has a very serious obligation. We have been exploiting Africa in a shameful way and we owe her a debt which we must now repay. We must pay back that which we have taken away. In order to start from a specific point, the Gen went to a particular people in Africa, the Bangwa people of Fontem in Cameroon. What did they go there for? Certainly not to distribute alms, but to give the Bangwa people the concrete means which will enable them to express themselves according to their own culture.

Only later on, while still continuing to help the Bangwa people, the Gen proceeded in this same spirit to bring the word of God to the other African countries. We can see the fruits already. Young people are flocking to Fontem from the Ivory Coast, from the Central African Republic, from Tanzania, and from Zaire.

Silvana: Alongside this pilot project, which the Gen call "Operation Africa," there developed other projects such as "Operation Feliciano" in Argentina, "Operation Tondo" in the Philippines and "Operation Mocambos" in Brazil. Then there are the small group projects. The Swiss Gen, for example, give everything they have to help the Gen of Brazil. And also, on an individual basis, the Gen give concrete help to whomever they meet, even to complete strangers, in whom they see Christ in need of help.

Peppuccio: It seems to me that what we have just told you is a real contribution toward helping the needy in the twentieth century. The starting point for solving our enormous social problems in an authentic way must be this: to build new relationships based on respect for the way of thinking of the other, who may see the same problems but sees them in a different way. It is said, for example, that imperialistic attitudes of every kind must be overcome, and this certainly includes those that make us impose on others certain social solutions because we think they are the only right ones.

Not A Faction Among Others

Q.: Today we are living in the midst of a great debate about structures which are outmoded and, therefore, under esamination. It is an ideological and political debate, in which the young people are not only involved, but are also taking a leading part. What is the role of the Gen in this debate and what do they have to say to their non-Christian and non-believing companions?

Peppuccio:, The Gen have a basic law which is "to love." It is therefore in this spirit that they try to be part of this debate. In other words, they do not enter it, as one faction alongside others, but as a unifying element to help draw out what is most positive and mutuallly valid in the contribution of other groups. The Gen know that in order to carry out this unifying and peacemaking role, they must place themselves above the level of the dispute on to that of the Gospel with all its human and divine implications.

"Operation Feliciano" in Northern Argentina. Since 1972 the Gen have spent their summer vacations building houses and other facilities in this underprivileged area.

"Operation Feliciano." The farewell party. More important than everything else was the personal rapport with people of different ages and social extraction. This has left a mark which goes beyond the material accomplishments.

Gen 3 Convention. The third generation of the Focolare Movement plays an important role in the spreading of the Gospel message among the young. Each one of these conventions has been conceived as a big five-day game with a different theme for every year. In 1975 it was the Beatitudes. The Gen have lived them, have presented them through drama, songs, and drawings.

On this evangelical level, the Gen are able to offer to those young people who are interested, the possibility to meet in groups divided into "worlds," as they say, to review together in depth all the problems they are concerned with. They study all problems — spiritual, economic, political, cultural and so on — in an evangelical attitude because, even though the Gospel does not contain a political message in itself, it is light which enlightens politics, as well as art, economics, and so on. For instance, we can already see the first fruits of this in a preliminary draft of Gen socio-economic guidelines drawn up by some French Gen in agreement with the other Gen.

They Answer with Facts

Q.: I think I can say with confidence, based on what you yourself just told me, that a purely verbal testimony of Christianity, a Christianity expressed in principles and in abstract notions, is totally rejected by today's youth. How do the Gen intend to bring factual proof of the truth they profess?

Silvana: From what we have just said, I think you can see that the characteristic of the Gen is just this: they answer with facts, with their lives. The Gen don't want to speak except when absolutely necessary. Therefore, no preaching, no sermons. If you look at their magazines, you will notice that ninety per cent of the contents are experiences. They do many things — draw, paint, act, sing, even talk, but all this is and all it wants to be is "life." I believe that the attraction many young people feel towards the Gen, when they are authentic, lies in the fact that they find life and not just words. After all, Jesus himself, whom the Gen want to imitate, began first by doing and only then turned to speaking.

Peppuccio: The word, if it is to be true, presupposes a life. We cannot forget that in the Holy Trinity, the Word is the Word of the Father and presupposes the existence of the Father. This is the Christian view of reality.

The Gen, too, want to follow this line. As Silvana said before, they speak little, but want to do much. The Gen know full well that the very structures of the Gen Movement, as well as every plan, every initiative, even the little attempt to draw up some socio-economic guidelines, can have value only inasmuch as they come from life and constantly refer back to life and are an expression of the experiences which the Gen are living together.

There is no age limit in living the spirituality of unity promoted by the Focolare. The Gen 4 (Fourth Generation) have their own programs in which they learn — in their own way — how to put the Gospel into practice.

The writer Igino Giordani, who was the first married man to become a focolarino, represents the Mass Movements within the Focolare Movement; he has been a source of inspiration for their birth.

4. THE FIRST MARRIED MAN TO BECOME A FOCOLARINO

Right in the old center of Rome, near the historic Piazza Navona, is the "Centro Uno," a center for ecumenical activities of the Focolare Movement. It is under the direction of Professor Igino Giordani, a distinguished figure in the Catholic cultural world, former deputy in the Italian Parliament, prolific writer, militant journalist, editor in chief of Città Nuova, *the Italian edition of* Living City. *No one, indeed, could be better qualified than Professor Igino Giordani to lead a dialogue with Christians of other denominations. As far back as 1927-28, when the first tentative advances were being made among the various Christian churches in the United States, he was the first Italian writer to be deeply involved in writing about ecumenical subjects. During that time, in fact, he lived and taught in the United States.*

But the reason for this interview is the fact that Igini Giordani was the first married man to become a Focolarino.

I knew from earlier conversations with him, that he had always seen the laity as existing within the Church and not at its edges. Giordani never accepted the idea of the laity as second-class citizens. This firm conviction of his has been nurtured and confirmed by the writings of the Church Fathers whom he had studied in great depth. "I recall," he told me once, "that after the days of the early Church, all kinds of distinctions began to grow up little by little — distinctions of class, of dress, of rules, even among religious — whereas I dreamt of a type of Christian who would go on living in the world, dressed in the way of the world and remaining in the fullness of family life, while at the same time working out his sanctification."

It was only after long years of searching and after different experiences that Igino Giordani found at last, in the Focolare Movement, a point where all the states in life meet and where the role of the Christian layperson in the Church and in the world was expressed as he desired. It is precisely on this most important topic that I asked him to tell me his story. Here it is.

Igino Giordani: My first meeting with what was to become the "Focolare Movement" (at the time it was simply called "Focolare of Unity") took place on September 17th, 1948, when some people came to see me at my office in the Parliament. There were three Franciscan Fathers, a young man, and a young woman. The young woman, Chiara Lubich, told me a story of a group of four or five young girls from Trent who had gotten together during the war to live with her a life consecrated to God. While all around them everything was crumbling beneath the ravages of war, they were at the service of those who suffered. That evening I wrote in my diary: "Gospel simplicity: atmosphere of paradise."

The daily reading of the Gospel, straight, without any embellishment, and of the missalette put these young girls in communion with God so that they actually lived with him in their home, a poor, bombed-out building. They went to him, not by complicated ways but by finding him in their own souls and in their brothers. Through the commandment of love which makes us one, they were seeking Jesus in the unity with one another. He had promised that he would be in the midst of whose who are united in his name.

These simple ideas, applied in such an unconditional way, astonished me. I had written books on religion and these people lived religion. They were consecrated to God with all the vows, although they went on living exteriorly as before — working in the home, in the school, in the shops and welcoming, without any formality, as many as wanted to live with God. In this way they repeated the miracle of St. Catherine of Siena, who had created outside the cloister a whole family of consecrated persons, made up of housewives and officials, priests and nuns, students, soldiers, and laborers.

The first men's Focolare opened in Trent in a garage.

The idea appealed to me because I had always wanted to live a religious life in the world, especially after reading the Fathers of the Church (Chrysostom, Augustine and Ambrose) who said that the Lord's call to sanctity was meant for everyone without distinction and that the lay people, including those who were married, should live like monks except for celibacy.

"Couldn't I be part of your community?" I asked. "Why not?" was the answer. "We want to be Christians as the Church wants us to be: to bear witness to Christ, that's all. You can do it too: come and join us."

Carlo de Ferrari, the unforgettable Archbishop of Trent, was quite surprised to see a member of Parliament join this small group of provincial people, whom almost nobody knew, and very few understood. The Archbishop, who had given his support to the Movement from the very beginning, became more and more its enthusiastic protector and guide. Often in writing to me, he would sign his letters, "Honorary Focolarino" or simply "Focolarino."

I also noticed how many other people changed from an initial attitude of perplexity to one of keen interest and even active participation, once they became acquainted with the spirit and the fruits of the Movement.

No Associate Members

On entering the Focolare, I finally fulfilled a vocation which I had felt for a long time. This was something I was not able to accomplish in other movements, even new ones, for they were more or less tied to a tradition which relegated the laity to a marginal position, almost like a spiritual proletariat, or as I've heard them called "associate members."

In the Focolare Ideal, there were no members, associate members, or non-members, but only human beings, all children of the one Father. The association with the Focolare was not limited to some prayers or devotions in common, but it was a permanent communion in which all were one, all mystically Christ, the Church. Day after day new people from all over were attracted, once the dividing walls had come down – young men and women, priests and nuns, people form every nation and walk of life. And since our aspiration was to win everyone to God, we welcomed agnostics and nonbelievers as well, uniting them, little by little, with a bond of charity.

The presence of a married man (and of a politician at that!) in the Focolare meant that the label of outsider no longer applied to someone blonging to a part of society which was commonly excluded from a life of virtue. His presence proved thet if a member of parliament could be converted, anyone could be converted. It created a breach in a long-standing social attitude and prejudice that was saturated with laicism and anticlericalism. The charity that had come from the Focolare recreated the spiritual bond between laity and priesthood and, as a consequence, between the profane and the sacred, the world and the Church, marriage and virginity. It helped rebuild a community where all differences vanished in the fire of charity.

Once the news spread, quite a few members of the Italian Parliament joined in, among whom were Pacati, Roselli and Foresi, whose son was to become a priest in the Focolare and, later on, the ecclesiastical assistant of the Movement. Once, even Premier De Gasperi came to see us, after having met us by chance in Fregene in 1949. He said that he was sorry he could not stay for dinner because of urgent state affairs (shortages of bread, threats of upheaval in Italy). Nevertheless, after coming to visit us for what he said would be a brief visit, the conversation went on and on until late at night. As he said goodbye that night, he told me: "This morning I woke up with a sense of despair, but you have given me hope once more."

Celibates and Married People Together

There are many ways of belonging to the Movement, as Focolarini, Volunteers, friends. Consecrated lay people who are married can be Focolarini with the same duties and rights as the Focolarini who live in common. For them, as for the others, the first right is to love which, in practice, is to serve.

To a certain extent they too live a rule of perfection, professing the evangelical counsels. They commit themselves to practice them in a way appropriate to their own state in life: chastity, according to the Encyclical *Casti Connubii,* poverty, in offering their superfluous goods; obedience, within their family duties and their availability. Each married Focolarino belongs to a Focolare Center — even though he does not live in it — going there as often as he can and, above all, living and radiating its ideal.

With these married lay people in the Movement, there came families whose homes were like domestic churches, like Focolari. Even today, I am deeply moved by the letters I receive from parents expressing their enthusiasm for this new way of living together in homes where there is Martha as well as Mary, where action is prompted by contemplation, and where there is Jesus in the midst between parents and children, so that their work and suffering become raw material for building the kingdom of God. For years their daily activities are performed as a priestly function where the divine is infused into the human: into their professions, their work, their studies, their art and so on. Christ, the whole Christ, is all of us.

A communion of this kind can be described as an answer to misery with love, to politics with religion, as an injection of sanctity into environments which have become parched and barren. Once the lack of understanding and the differences have disappeared, a supernatural atmosphere of spiritual virginity enters into both our souls and our homes, a pure communion with the saints, so that even if we are assailed by work, illness, taxes, or scandal, we find the Holy Spirit circulating among us, returning us to joy and giving us a reason for existing. Before, we lived according to the lesser portion of our existence, the physical one. Now we live according to the greater, the essential one. In this way, pain itself becomes love, while we learn to remain in the midst of turmoil as free human beings. We are free in the sense that we are free from the power of evil, free with the liberty of the children of God, who no longer fear tyranny, oppression or the arrogance of the mighty.

This is the *living* Church, achieved not so much by writings and speeches as by the testimony of life, as can best be seen at the Mariapolis (the name for our summer gatherings). At one time these were held only in a mountain village in northern Italy. But later on, due to the ever-growing number of participants, the Mariapolis was held in different parts of the world. Mariapolis is a name which is inspired by and takes its rule from Mary, who was a virgin, and also a fiancée, wife, mother and a widow, and, as such, inspires this gathering of different people for one single purpose — to generate Christ in the world. Since all men are children of God, perhaps subconsciously harboring in their hearts a yearning for the Father, people of every walk of life came to these gatherings from the earliest beginnings. The first year there were seven persons, the second year there were two hundred, the third four thousand, and by the fourth year it had become a problem to accommodate everybody. "What did you do to grow in such incredible proportions and with such speed?" a parish priest from Trent asked me one day in 1951. "Well," I said, "we did some advertising." He burst out laughing because he knew that there was no advertising. Even I, who had been writing a few articles at the beginning, was advised to stop writing by Bishop De Ferrari.

In the same spirit we now are in fraternal contact with non-Catholics as well as with Anglicans, Greek Orthodox, Lutherans, Baptists, Episcopalians and even with non-Christians, Buddhists, Muslims and so on. Thus the Movement makes its contribution to the ministry of reconciliation through a universal ecumenism; it strives to establish peace in a world which has reached this alternative: unite or perish.

A Rediscovery of the Gospel

This social and religious apostolate (from politics to ecumenism, from family to youth) which is being carried out in homes, in workshops, in restaurants, at union headquarters, derives its norm from a series of movements which support and regulate its development. These are the Movement for a New Humanity, the New Family Movement, the New Parish Movement, which by their very names already indicate an updating and renewing of social structures and activities.

Also for priests and for men and women religious, there are movements suited to their needs. In the field of ecumenism, there is "Centro Uno" for the unity of Christians. I, myself, have occasion to enter into relationships with heads of many churches in many countries in the conviction that the unity of Christians, or better, of believers, is a leaven to heal social structures worn away by individualism and discord, by war and racism, by fear and rivalry. This, too, is a spontaneous fruit of that "ideal of charity" which is the reason-for-being of the Focolare Movement.

Time and again I have seen that in people who were troubled by the fast pace of change in our time, the Movement leads to a rediscovery of the Gospel, a need for the Church, a communion with God, "This is the proof that God really exists," they often say. Simple and joyous expressions of Christianity by the youth, often expressed in songs and music by the Gen bands and by the cordiality of their solidarity, are the luminous note of life in the deadly night of disunity. It is no wonder that the great majority of this family which now includes people of all races and is spread over all the continents, is made up of young people. With them, we older ones, after being rescued from our depressing solitude, are compelled to experience a daily rebirth of our spirits and youthfully overcome boredom and death. These young people do not turn away from life by escaping into the hypnosis of drugs, but heroically embrace the cross and accept the "gift of suffering" in order to serve humanity. Heroism: this is the impression we older people have when looking at these girls and boys. I remember the disappointment of a well-known cardinal, now dead, as he spoke about the lack of understanding that this heroic behavior was met with by many people in the world. I answered that this was the fate of all works of God, but I noted that such musunderstanding highlights the boldness of these young creatures, many of whom come from well-to-do families and were headed towards successful careers, but who have given up everything to serve others.

And now let me bear witness to one evident truth: the animating force of this enormous and rapid evolution from a tiny provincial nucleus to a multitude which has spread throughout the universal Church, was and is Chiara Lubich. Having consecrated herself to God as a young girl, she brought to the Movement the ingenuity of God's love to build souls and works, to understand and receive the most beautiful aspirations, in order to direct the currents of history toward the house of the Father, a house in which death is dead.

5. "VOLUNTEERS" FOR A NEW HUMANITY

The fifth appointment in my series of interviews took me to Grottaferata near Rome. Here is situated the office of the New Humanity Movement, a most interesting expression of the Focolare Movement. Its purpose is to contribute to an evangelical renewal of humanity, in all its various fields of endeavor, what we call "worlds": the worlds of education, politics, business and labor; the worlds of art, medicine, social service, and so on.

The "Volunteers" are the backbone of this movement. At Grottaferrata, I interviewed Giulio Marchesi, an engineer and one of the individuals responsible for the New Humanity Movement, and Claretta Dal Ri, who heads the women's section of the Volunteers.

Organizations and a Way of Living

Q.: We live in a time of democracy. It is a time when daily events encourage every citizen to join particular parties, or groups, or organizations among the many that can be found in our political and social lives. Since the

New Humanity Movement, which was born of the Focolare, has to live in this reality, what is its attitude toward it? That is, can the members of all the different parties and organizations of different ideological leanings belong to the New Humanity Movement?

Giulio: I think it would be good to go over a few things that have already been said in preceding interviews. The Focolare Movement is a movement embodying a spirituality. It was born and exists in order to bring, in its own way, the Gospel into the world. Although it is a movement that has many diverse vocations in it, it has never taken, nor does it ever wish to take, in any of its many facets, the form of a political party, or labor union, or any other association. Its members, however, are not restricted from doing so on a personal basis. In fact, they do exactly this and they actively work to bring to these organizations, as I will explain later on, the spirit of the Movement. Its members wish to collaborate with everyone, including those of different faiths, to bring about an end result which is just and good.

Perhaps it is better first to clarify the nature of the New Humanity Movement. It seems to me that the "political and social dynamics" or activities, nurtured by the associations that you mentioned, are a way of "being society" and of regulating the human society. They are not, however, the only way. Every now and then, I notice in these activities signs of profound crisis, disillusionment, and serious gaps that, as the situation stands, cannot be bridged. Humanity, today, is searching in other ways to be itself. Many attempts in all directions are being made. I think that the interview about the New Humanity Movement should develop along these lines.

I have already said that ours is a movement with a spirituality at its basis. It is not a political association, not even in the New Humanity Movement, which is one of its many expressions and the one that most deeply penetrates into worldly realities. Don't think, however, that the whole thing is up in the air, so indefinite as to be beyond reality, and quite out of touch with the concrete realities in which we live.

On the contrary, the Focolare Movement did not come from a study of the Gospel, but rather from a daily discovery of what is contained there — a discovery that the first Focolarine made by putting the Gospel into practice. Its contents were words of life that they were able to penetrate profoundly only by living them. This discovery had a transforming effect. As they communicated to others this realization, the first little group, almost without any explicit intention, grew larger and spread out. In other words, a social body was spontaneously being formed which is very widespread today. At the beginning, in its very seed, it already constituted a new society; new also is its worldly and temporal behavior.

You already know the story of the Movement's origin, so I won't repeat it. I will go on, instead, to the latest chapter. The members who are now living everywhere throughout the world, and especially those directly involved in the life of our society, are people of our time. They have families, they work, they participate in recreational activities. They make all kinds of social, political, labor, and welfare commitments. They experience, as others do, the demands, difficulties, crises, and hopes of today's society. They also feel strongly (because they experience it daily in the new society which the Focolare Movement, with all its limitations and defects, is striving to be) that the lived message of the Gospel offers them a very different way of being men today, of living together among men, not only in Paradise but even on earth, not just in church but even at the bank, in the factory, in the hospital, and so on.

Hence, at a certain moment, came the awareness that all these people, since they are involved in the realities of this world, could exercise a transforming influence on civil society — not only an individual and sporadic influence, but the influence of a mass movement — if they were united among themselves and with others in resolving their social problems in the evangelical spirit they had already experienced.

You ask: Can people belonging to organizations with different ideologies also belong to the New Humanity Movement? The New Humanity Movement is not an organization in the strict sense of the word, but rather, a vital movement, a way of living. Will the people of whom you speak accept such a life? If they accept it, they reject, perhaps without even yet realizing it, all those theoretical aspects of their ideologies that are in opposition to the Gospel. We certainly don't turn these people away. Nor do we disguise the truth so that it won't be recognized. We lead our normal lives, and he who is not against us is with us.

This collaboration among different persons is possible because the New Humanity Movement works on another level. It does not antagonize other groups. Its members, while living and working with others to advance the whole political community, seek to establish a new spirit in them, one that is able to overcome the barriers brought on by the innumerable divisions of today's society. In this way, all may live in a more human atmosphere, an atmosphere where that which unites is the prevailing force, and where partisanship is overcome by re-establishing good and true goals, which are the reason we are together.

Q.: Besides generalizing about the nature of the society proposed by the New Humanity Movement, can you give me some specific examples of the results that have been attained?

Claretta: Certainly. In a small hospital, some doctors, nurses, sisters, attendants, the chaplain, the emergency room personnel, and the switchboard operator all arrived at a deep understanding which brought about a change in their former attitudes, so that the common center of their lives in the hospital became the patient. The patient is no longer a number, or a clinical case, but a man, who, from the time he arrives in the admitting office or in the Emergency room, finds a smile and a friendly face. He is recognized as a person who has other problems besides his medical problem. He has a family, for instance, and this is where the switchboard operator plays a very important role to keep the communications open and friendly and convenient. At the same time, new kinds of relationships are

Chicago, June 13, 1976. Different moments of the New Humanity Convention sponsored by the Chicago Volunteers. The participants, scattered in two groups, discussed and shared experiences regarding the worlds of education, business, and industry.

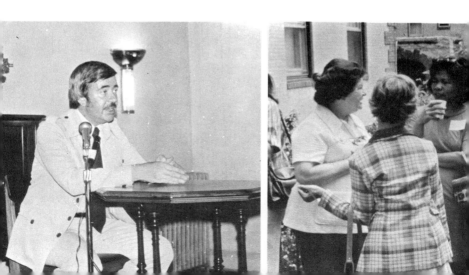

New Humanity Convention in Chicago. Workshops and sharing during the day. The Volunteers of the Focolare feel very strong the call to bring the Gospel into the structures of society through their lives.

developed for this patient with the personnel within the hospital.

In another case, the manager of an industrial consultant firm felt he ought to establish a new relationship with his subordinates. He decided that everyone should have the opportunity to participate in the running of the company, including participation in the develpment of plans for more efficient working conditions. He even introduced a system of profit sharing.

Elsewhere, the director of a national corporation is taking special care of the organization of his workers. He personally meets with his staff of four hundred, even though they are located in two different cities. He visits them on the job, and together they evaluate the work that has been done and decide what changes should be made for improvement. Both management and labor are finding satisfaction in the results.

Again, in the process of collective bargaining, this spirit which is shared by people in traditionally opposed positions of power, made the difference. Some union leaders and workers in a medium-sized industrial plant got together with the employer and the production manager to work out a new way of determining salary levels in the lower income brackets. Disregarding the previous antagonistic policies of the union and of the company, they managed to achieve an agreement. In fact, new criteria of evaluation were brought into their negotiations that showed a greater concern for the worker as a human being. This agreement was later adopted as a model for the negotiations in similar companies.

Two French businessmen felt that they should plan their business affairs not in terms of commodities but in terms of people. In short, they felt that business should become a real "service." They interested other businessmen in this idea. Even though these other men didn't share their Christian outlook, they accepted its human dimension. A strong spiritual bond developed among a number of them. With another forty or so who symphathized with this idea, a plan for economic reorganization was drawn up. The whole organization − in its various aspects of economics, advertising, urban planning, etc. − had as its center the human being and not the profit motive. This held true for all its various dealings with customers, with the businessmen among themselves, with those involved in large corporations as well as in small businesses. Of course, there has been a lot of opposition to this plan, for it contradicts the rules of a consumer society. In the city where this project is taking place, everyone is either "pro" or "con" about the "spirit of Chamnord" (Chamnord is the name of the project).

Another thing, a lot is being done among those in need. As an example, I can mention a project, led by two of our friends in a city of northern Germany, to bring the old people out of isolation and give them a value in society. The experiment was written up by the local press, and then later on taken as a model by the regional government.

Regarding the Third World, it's not necessary to repeat the experiences that we have already made in the "Mocambos" (slums) in Recife, a northeastern city of Brazil, in the Philippines, and in other places. Nor will I repeat what you already know about the Bangwa people in the town of Fontem in Cameroon where members of the Movement and natives, both Christian an non-Christian, live together in a completely new type of community.

Our Presence in the Working World

Q.: Has the "Ideal" of the Focolarini found equal acceptance on all social levels? Does it appeal to the poorer people as it does to the middle and upper classes? Has the "message" of the Focolarini reached the right wavelength for communicating with the whole working world? Or is it that the working world keeps itself distant, suspecting that this Movement also is made of people who — however noble their intention to re-establish a living faith, a life of love and unity — don't really show themselves to be in touch with today's society?

Giulio: The first Focolarine were nearly all school teachers or simple clerks. The first male members were two manual workers and a painter. Afterwards people of all social classes joined the Movement. Today, in the Movement, which includes Focolarini, Volunteers, Gen, and the mass movements (I won't include the Religious in this group), you can find people in all professions and jobs.

At this very time, for example, at the Mariapolis Center in Rocca di Papa, there are meetings of Focolare members each week. I'm often invited because one of the topics talked about frequently is the New Humanity Movement.

The experiences are many and different. Some experiences come from people who work in factories, others from construction workers, and many from those who are in management. There is a continous growth of our presence in the working world. In addition, the workers who are part of our Movement are not there simply following the crowd. Rather, they are the ones who very often serve as stimuli to other workers.

The evangelical spirit animating the Movement leads it also to work with the underprivileged and the handicapped, who are, for the most part, the most defenseless members of our society.

Moreover, it can be noted that the life awakened by this spirit and the communion among people from different social extractions and nationalities enriches and refines one's soul. Very often, as a result of this life, it is difficult to distinguish the social background of those who are involved in the Movement.

Therefore, the Movement is open to all. Men are men and all must be loved as brothers, each in his own way, even though we logically have a preference for those more in need and we find that it is with the rich that we have the greatest difficulty. But even here we have to say that the few rich people who have followed the evangelical counsel and who have given everything to the poor, are among the most committed in the Movement. It is good to be open to everyone. We can do this because we have no political philosophy which forces us to make choices.

The Great Attraction Today

This is the great attraction today: to reach the highest contemplation while sharing in the life of every man; one man among many.

I would say more: to merge oneself with the crowd so as to allow the divine to penetrate it, like wine penetrates a piece of bread.

I would say even more: as sharers in God's plans for mankind, to pattern points of light within the crowd, sharing shame, hunger, troubles, and brief joys with our neighbor.

The attraction today, as in all times, is Jesus and Mary: the highest conceivable expression of the human and the divine.

The Word of God, a carpenter's son; the Seat of Wisdom, a mother at home.

Chiara Lubich
(from *Meditations*)

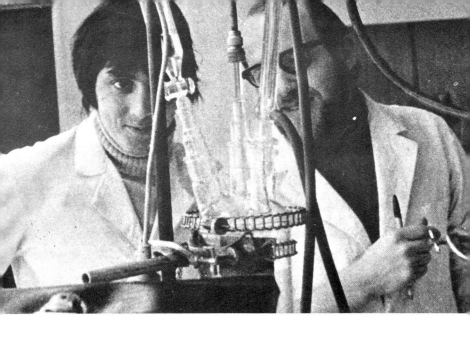

Above: **Besancon, France.** Because of the presence of a Volunteer, a new and spontaneous understanding exists among students and professors.
Below: **São Paulo, Brazil.** An accounting office where the manager, a Volunteer, has brought about important changes in rapport among people and in the office structures. The sharing of the profits and the new set-up of the business have deeply transformed the internal situation of the office, giving everyone the chance to be fulfilled and therefore to become co-responsible.

To Change Men and Structures

Q.: It has been said that the crisis of today's world is the crisis of man and of structures. It is obvious that the New Humanity Movement agrees that there is a "crisis of man." But does it share the view that there is a crisis of structures? And if it does, what does the Movement do, Claretta, to renew structures, besides renewing men? Does it act concretely in this situation?

Claretta: It is true that today's crisis is also one of structures. The two things are bound together. As a result, we hold that it is necessary to exert an influence in both directions by helping both men and structures to change.

What do we do concretely for the structures? The members of the New Humanity Movement do not want to bring this change about by themselves. Instead, they belong to organizations that work to give new structures to society. They make their active contributions in schools, in unions, in legislatures, in health care units, and so on.

We are aware, however, that there are cases where the structures themselves are not in need of change so much as the method of using them.

All this, as you can see, comes both from those among us who are directly responsible for the changing of structures at various levels and also from the influence exerted by the Movement as a whole.

It is important to regard structures not as rigid schemes possessing an absolute value, but rather as instruments continually being modified to meet the changing needs of man.

Furthermore, those who belong to the New Humanity Movement are also in contact with other members throughout the world, and this helps them greatly to have a broad and more complete outlook on the issues they deal with.

The Role of the "Volunteers"

Q.: In this process of renewing men and their social structures, what is the function of the Volunteers? Isn't there a danger that the Volunteers, who draw inspiration from a deep but very definite experience of spiritual renewal, will act as an exclusive group rather than collaborate with all "men of good will," as Pope John called those who are working to make the world worthy of mankind.

Claretta: I think we are far removed from any such idea since we are fully convinced that the human society will be renewed by the contribution of all and that we learn something good from everyone.

In order to answer your question, perhaps it is wise to explain who the Volunteers are, and what they represent in the Focolare Movement.

The primary characteristic of the Volunteers is that they are committed laypersons. As laypersons they strongly desire to incarnate the spirit of the Movement in all aspects of human life, from the most simple to the most complex, and they do this both individually or in groups. The Volunteers live the full range of human realities (political, economic, social, artistic, educational, etc.) and consider them as means to re-evangelize themselves and the society they live in.

On the other hand, it is that very profound, spiritual experience of renewal of which you spoke that makes them suitable for the task. And here allow me to emphasize the importance of this spiritual experience which is, after all, the same spirit of the entire Focolare Movement. This experience, while it touches each member personally, always tends to create a brotherly rapport and, therefore, it is lived as a "body."

Spontaneously, then, this spiritual experience expresses itself everywhere in creating the "family," the "community," making it visible through works of mutual charity — hospitality, mutual help, etc. — to the point that one is compelled to exclaim, "See how they love one another . . ."

And it follows too that in the "family" there is a complete and open communication of all the news, which the imagination of love makes varied and rich. Thus a communion of both spiritual and material goods comes about spontaneously, and these goods can be anything from free time to fruits of learning, from intellectual talents to material goods.

The "communion of goods" is practiced by each one in many different ways, even to the point of giving not only what is surplus, but also what is necessary. This has become the norm for the Volunteers, though with the utmost freedom, and thus it takes on an ever more absolute meaning. Little by little, this communion of goods penetrates families, environments, and so on. It encourages every one to let the needs of others, of each neighbor, enter into and determine his own personal "economy." As you can see, this creates a new life style and something more.

I say this to emphasize how deep such a spiritual experience is, and at the same time how it is always open to others. Besides, the ideal that inspires the Movement is "that all may be one."

This spirit is open to all; it doesn't impose a certain way of life on others. On the contrary, it enables each one to be more and more a presence of love beside every other person, that is, one who values all that is true, beautiful and good. In a word, this spirit values all that is positive in every individual and in every group. This includes suffering, failure, and poverty, which are so much despised in our times. I could continue on this topic indefinitely.

Since this is the spirit that animates the Volunteers, you will understand more easily their role in the New Humanity Movement. They are like the leaven in the process of renewal of men and structures. I don't wish to be presumptuous, but keeping in mind all our limitations, the sincerity of this commitment makes me think of the magnificent Letter to Diognetus written in the second century: "The difference between Christians and the rest of mankind is not a matter of nationality, or language, or customs. Christians do not live apart in separate cities of their own, nor speak any special dialects, nor practice any eccentric way of life. . . . They pass their lives in whatever township — Greek or foreign — each man's lot has determined; and conform to ordinary local usage in their clothing, diet and other habits. Nevertheless, the organization of their community does exhibit some features that are remarkable, and even surprising. To put it briefly, the relation of Christians to the world is that of a soul to the body."

Our Politics

Q.: It has happened to me several times that someone has taken me aside to say, "Listen, let me ask you something. What is the political goal of the Focolarini? I finally have a chance to turn the question over to someone qualified to answer it.

Giulio: I'll answer you with another question. What do you mean by political goal? Do you mean a sort of party line, a government policy for a particular country, such as might be advanced by a political party? In this sense, obviously since we are not a political party but a spiritual movement, we do not have a political goal of our own. The Movement has spread throughout the world and it would be a mistake to try to impose the same political ideas on countries which are quite different from one another.

But if, instead, when you say " political goal" you mean something more general, though no less concrete, if you mean a set of principles from which our members can draw inspiration so that they may act, each according to his own circumstances, then yes, of course, we have a political goal. This is exactly what the members of the New Humanity

Movement, who take part in different political associations, seek to apply, keeping in mind the particulars of their own countries and giving value to whatever is good in the thoughts and actions of everyone — including non-Christians.

What is this political goal in a broad sense?

It is the message of the Gospel, either forgotten or little known, and even less lived. Men, because they are the children of the same Father, who is Love, are brothers and must love each other. That is, they must find fulfillment of their individual personalities not by exalting themselves, but by losing themselves and by giving themselves to others. I am sure that you remember the words of St. Paul when he compares Christians — all united as members of a body whose head is Christ — to the human body. We are all part of the same body, each in his own place, each with his own reason for existing at the service of others. Therefore, the stronger members take care of the weaker ones; but all work with the strength of the charity that comes from God.

Now it is necessary that this body, which is the Church, made in the likeness of the Trinity and through the participation in its divine life, reach out to society and make of it, too, a body bound together and animated by love. Please take note that this does not mean to impose a religious view on those who do not have faith, but it is instead a rediscovery of the true nature and the profound need which is in all men. I say this because I have had this experience myself in these years in the Focolare Movement.

Here we have stated only briefly parts of what could be a very long discussion. Nevertheless, the few and simple words that I have shared with you bear directly upon the fundamental problems of everyday life in our society: such as the difficulties of reconciling authority and freedom, which lie at the basis of every political theory; and the problems of property, which divide economic doctrines; and those of equality and inequality among men, upon which social solutions are based.

Naturally, as you get down to the details, the unity of the general plan takes on, little by little, multiple and diversified expressions in accordance with local conditions and with the tendencies of individual men. God has not muzzled men — nor will we — with dogmatically determined concrete solutions. He has left us free, free to search, to make new attempts, and to arrive at solutions on our own. But above all, God has left us free to discover that we need one another and, after all has been said and done, free to love one another as brothers born into the same family.

Do you think that words such as these sound naive and useless in the jungle we live in? How do you think the demands of the first trade union organizers sounded to the industrialists of the last century? The important thing is that whatever is said should come from vital needs and experiences. If it is so, sooner or later it will be acknowledged by all.

6. PRIESTS, OF COURSE,
BUT FIRST OF ALL CHRISTIANS

In a wooded area above the town of Frascati, near Rome, lies St. Francis House. It is where the School of Formation for the Priests' Branch of the Focolare Movement is situated. At the time of my visit, diocesan priests and seminarians from different continents were attending the school. I met with Fr. Silvano Cola who is responsible for the Priests' School.

Q.: Every so often, I hear about meetings in Grottaferrata for members of the particular branch of the Focolare spirituality called the Priests' Movement. I am told that these meetings are attended by as many as five or six hundred priests at a time and that in Germany last January, there were two hundred and fifty priests, together with twenty Lutheran ministers among the participants. I also know that the Movement has meetings even in Brazil with more than one hundred and twenty priests and some bishops; this is especially striking since the situation there is such as hardly to warrant the possibility of getting four or five together under the same roof. Considering things as they are today, these events are impressive, to say the least.

Fr. Silvano: The great number of participants at our meetings astonishes us also. Recently, at a meeting held at the Mariapolis Center in Rocca di Papa, there were eight hundred priests from all over Europe; and what you have

Frascati, Italy. Some of the priests who have taken part in the "School of Formation" sponsored by the Priests' Movement within the Focolare. Coming from all over the world, they spend six months there. They are gathered in small communities in order to have a strong experience of the "New Commandment."

Above: **Priests at the School of formation in Frascati.**
Landscaping a soccerfield. The program of each day
includes prayer, study, and work in an atmosphere of
deep unity.
Below: **This old Capuchin Monastery,** in Frascati,
Italy, once the cradle of Capuchin Missions, now mod-
ernized in the interiors to serve as. School of Formation for Priests, has become a center radiating an
intense spiritual renewal among priests.

just said about the meeting in Ottmaring, Germany, is also correct. The German press, which covered the event, could not help but express a certain amazement. It was the same for Brazil where one meeting of priests was visited by fifteen bishops, who were very happy with what they saw.

These meetings and conventions are held several times a year, in every country where there are centers of the Focolare Movement. This gives you an idea of the impact that the Movement's spirituality has had on the diocesan clergy.

There are also the Gens, that is, the Gen Seminarians who make up quite a sizeable Movement of their own. They publish their own magazine, *GENS,* which has a circulation of 3,500 copies.

Our Priests' Movement, I would say parenthetically, is just one of the many movements and associations for priests which have come into being in these last few years. It shows that even in the midst of so many difficulties, the Church is experiencing a new blossoming vitality far stronger than one would think.

You asked me, however, to speak to you about the Priests' Movement connected with the Focolare. From the very beginning of the Focolare Movement, many priests have been struck by its spirituality which, we could say, is nothing else but the Gospel lived to the fullest in today's world.

Beyond the Crisis

Q.: Obviously it continues to impress many priests, even now, during this crisis in the priesthood. I would like to ask you some questions about this crisis, since you have so much experience and are an exponent of the Priests' Movement. It seems that a consequence of the secularization and protest of our days is a mentality leading many to believe that nothing is certain anymore. Everyone seems to be seeking answers, or better, a new lifestyle. The so-called priestly identity seems to have been lost. How do those involved in the Priests' Movement diagnose this serious spiritual suffering? What kind of therapy would you suggest to cure it?

Fr. Silvano: For the diagnosis, we have to go back somewhat in time. Let us take a look at the clergy of the forties. Their official position appeared to be still fairly solid and respected. The personal situation of each priest, however, was different. In those days, it was already being undermined by an interior sense of dissatisfaction. The ideal image of priestly life that seminarians had envisaged for themselves would crumble in the first years of their ministry since they found themselves caught up in a life that often became routine. There is no sense repeating what everybody already knows. Perhaps I can explain with an analogy.

Have you ever read the story by Luigi Pirandello of a well-known professor who, having ruined his eyesight by pouring over book after book, finally presents the fruits of his long years of study to a huge classroom filled with empty coats? The analogy may not be perfect, but the meaning, that is, the gap existing between priests and congregations, is pretty much the same. You can imagine, therefore, the sense of uneasiness experienced by many priests. I do not think, as many believe, that 1968 was the year in which the clergy began to protest. It came out into the open then, but it already existed in the fifties as a deep-seated dramatic rebellion by many young priests.

Then, along came the Focolare Movement, by chance it seemed. We priests came face to face with these young lay people who were truly living evangelical lives. Suddenly, it was as if Jesus had come back on earth to warn us, "How terrible for you, too, teachers of the Law! You put loads on men's backs which are hard to carry, but you yourselves will not stretch out a finger to help them carry those loads." (Luke 12:46). Do you understand what I mean? They were actually living the Gospel while we were preaching it. They were happy even in carrying their cross, while we were desperate, with or without the cross, since, in our despair, we did not recognize the cross. They seemed to be real persons because they loved, and we felt like bureaucrats.

I would not want you to think, however, that this was true for all. I do not want to generalize, but it is a fact that many of us discovered that we were priests without being — and I mean it in a dynamic sense — Christians. In substance, this seems to me to be the spiritual anguish you mentioned.

And for a therapy? Do you know what it means to

discover Jesus? It means that you discover again that Christianity has a fascination, and that you are alive after having been dead. In a certain sense, you feel that what is essential is to be, so to say, another Jesus first, and then, a priest. I have seen among the Focolarini how secondary it is to them to be a doctor, or an architect, or whatever, because this is not the essential. Later, you realize that being a priest is also a beautiful thing, but your values are no longer confused. After all, Jesus was a priest because he was Jesus; he was not Jesus because he was a priest.

The Joy of Reliving the Adventure of Jesus

Q.: It seems like a rather "shocking" discovery and I don't think it made life any easier for you. Can you tell me something about what happened next?

Fr. Silvano: Certainly, with these new ideas and with the revolution they brought into our private and public lives, I must admit that we were reather frowned upon in those days. I'm talking about the years between 1950 and 1952. People kept asking us, "What do you want?" We would answer that we didn't want anything except to be Christians as were the Focolarini. Of course, we spent as much of our free time as we could with them, trying to live as they did. Imagine what it meant for us to be all together, to love and help one another with joy, because we wanted to live mutual love and to see Jesus in each other. We no longer felt a certain nostalgia for Jesus, because he was present among us. He was the meeting point for our souls, the brother par excellence who gives meaning and value to our whole existence.

Yet some people thought all this was a deviation from our priestly ideal. They looked at us with diffidence, to say the least. Actually, I can't deny that, in a way, they were right because, at times, our attitude showed all the lack of restraint of neophytes. In 1960, something happened that can only be explained through God's imagination. At that time, there were about four hundred priests who adhered to the spirituality of the Focolare Movement. Suddently, they were forbidden not only to belong to the Movement, but also to attend any of its meetings. It was this very fact, in a way, that marked the beginning of the Priests' Branch of the Focolare Movement. In order to continue our experience, we were obliged to meet among ourselves. In other words, instead of leaning on the Focolarini, we had to be like them.

In 1962, when the prohibition was lifted, we discovered that we had become a small body within the Focolare Movement. We were distinct from the other branches, yet we were living the same reality, just as in a family with different members each has his own personality, yet all are brothers. As a Movement, we felt more of a family than ever before.

Now we are many, but of course not all have the same degree of commitment. The majority absorb the spirituality, try to live it and give it to the others. They take part in the get-togethers in order to renew themselves after the inevitable accumulation of dust from being in the world.

There are others, however, for whom this is not enough. They are and remain diocesan priests, but they want to live together with other priests in the same way as the Focolarini. Wherever possible, they try to live together in a rectory which then becomes a Focolare of priests. They live evangelical poverty. You have already written about the Focolarini, however, so I will not repeat what you have already said.

Q.: Tell me something about what you say to all these priests. What do they find that is so rewarding in these meetings?

Fr. Silvano: We tell them our experience. As you know, the Focolarini always begin recounting the story of the Movement by saying, "It was a time of war and everything was crumbling around us. . . ." Well, simply change a few words and you have the story of many priests today. "It was a time of protest and changes and everything in the Church seemed to be crumbling.' Most priests today experience darkness, confusion, anguish, or a sense of failure. This can be a grace, however, because it makes it easier to find God in a very real way. This was the experience of the first Focolarine. Without going back and retelling the whole story of the Focolare Movement and its spirituality, I can tell you from experience that in it, there are certain characteristics in which everyone, and especially a priest, can recognize himself.

Do you know what is most impressive about our meet ings? It is the fact that we simply tell the priests to stop analyzing everything in terms of theology. We ask them not to theorize about the very experience they are having, nor to try to make an exegesis of the Gospel's words. We encourage them, rather, to live fully an experience of unity, of Jesus in our midst, "Where two or three . . ." and to put the Gospel into practice. This is a lot to ask of priests, but if they take the step, they find a deep joy, they experience a new freedom. They lose a theology that is made of words and rediscover the joy of living the adventure of Jesus. Once we are at this point, the crisis of identity no longer exists.

No More Isolation

Q.: If you do not mind, I would like to continue on this subject of the "crisis." There is no doubt that there is also a psychological wound. There seems to be a certain discomfort that is caused by isolation, which, at times, leads some priests to seek their own individual solution. However, these solutions are not and can never be fully satisfying. These priests, on the one hand, do not find their place in the ordinary context of society. And, on the other hand, they end up losing sight of their original purpose. Can you tell me how the Priests" Movement faces this dramatic psychological problem? Does the Priests' Movement have an answer for it?

Fr. Silvano: The problem of solitude really doesn't exist for us. If anything, the opposite is true. You already know that the spirituality of the Focolare Movement is by nature communitarian because it is based on, "where two or three are united in my name . . . ." What does this mean? It means that individualism is banned from the very beginning. From this you can see that, besides everything else, it is an up-to-date way of life.

I'll give you an example. Let's take the situation of two or three priests living in a parish. They share the same home, but their living together could be merely functional. That is to say, that it is dictated by their pastoral duties. Each one fulfills his specific task, makes his own decisions, takes on his own initiatives, often without having any rapport or spiritual communion with the others. Of course, this does not solve the problem of isolation. It can actually make it worse than before. We have to ask ourselves, "Where did things go wrong?" I think it is precisely in a reversal of values. When St. Peter urges that in the first place there must be mutual and constant charity, he means that even the pastoral mission takes second place to this Christian duty. What, after all, is the purpose of pastoral work, if not to bring the kingdom of God among men so that all men become part of the new family which Jesus came to establish on earth? It is a family where each one must be ready to give his life for the other. What kind of a kingdom can we bring if we do not first live this charity ourselves, if we have no experience of it, or if our own life does not coincide with what we teach?

Let's take two or three priests who want, first of all, to be united among themselves, and who, therefore, are ready to sacrifice their own ideas, since mutual charity is greater than all the ideas of the world. They are priests who want to live evangelical poverty so as not to fall back into a comfortable middle-class life. They want to keep their hearts free from any personal attachments because that, too, is a way of possessing something, and it hinders a total communion. These two or three priests, in other words, want somehow to live mutual love as we know it exists among the persons of the Holy Trinity. Now, isn't this what Jesus wants from us? Listen to this quotation from one of the greatest theologians who lived four centuries ago, and then tell me if it doesn't describe perfectly the experience of the first Focolarine, which has become the focal point of the Movement's spirituality. Commenting on Jesus' words, "Where two or three . . ." this is what the theologian said, "The presence of Jesus among those united in his name produces the same effect that his physical presence produced when he was among his disciples." Now, you can't imagine, for instance, that Peter was thinking about his wife when he was with Jesus. In this sense, we can understand priestly celibacy. During one of our meetings a few months ago, one of the married Lutheran ministers told all of us present that, after his experience, he could understand why the Catholic Church maintains celibacy for her priests. He commented, "The love among you is greater than that which has ever existed between my wife and me."

Now, multiply this relationship by five hundred or a thousand priests all over the world, and then add to it the communion of goods, to the point where a priest in one of the most isolated and poorest communities in Northeast Brazil will have no less and no more than one of our German priests who, being previously better off, has given up part of his goods.

We must also add to this the sharing of news and experiences, not only among us priests, but with the entire Focolare Movement with whom we form a single family. Top it off with the hundreds of other inventions that are the fruit of mutual love and which keep the supernatural bond strong and lasting. Tell me, can you still talk about isolation?

The Leadership of the Cross

Q.: If my impressions are correct, it seems that there is also another factor which makes the priest wonder about his identity. In other words, (forgive me if in expressing my questions, I may sound a bit straightforward) up until fairly recently, the priest was a highly respected civil, as well as religious, leader. He had a certain social status. The civil leadership is all but gone now. The religious leadership seems to be in a pretty shaky condition, with the exception of those cases where an individual priest has a talent for it. On the other hand, a young priest was once telling me, "to be an efficient leader, you must be born one; one doesn't become a leader only because he is told that he is one." With the apparent loss of these two leaderships, priests have seen the traditional values which were linked to their earlier status in society vanish. They seem to be asking themselves, "Who and what are we now?" As of yet, they have no answer to what their role is. What is your answer, Father Silvano? How can the Priests' Movement heal this social gap and what is the role of priests today according to you?

Fr. Silvano: The question deserves a long answer. I can tell you briefly what has been our experience. Trying to remain true to the spirituality of the Focolare Movement, we have aimed only at one leadership, the leadership that, as a priest, Jesus had. It was said of him, in fact, that "his royal throne was the cross." It is the leadership he himself had chosen when he exclaimed, "When I will be raised up, I will draw all people to myself." You might object, saying that this solution is a little too spiritualistic and seems to evade the historical problem. I assure you, however, that it is a reality with many social implications. We have experienced that when two or three priests try to live in unity, which means a continuous dying to oneself, what Jesus promised — that is, "that the world will believe" — really happens. After all, wasn't the Church born from the cross? We have seen, and continue to see, that the unity of two or more gives birth to the Christian community. You witnessed it yourself in Trent more than thirty years ago, when you saw the community that blossomed around the first group of girls. This phenomenon repeats itself constantly wherever there is a Focolare. It is such a powerful reality that from it we understood what the key to our ministry had to be. It is in this way that the New Parish Movement came to life. But I imagine this will be the topic of your next interview.

Q.: That's right. I'd like to know, instead, why in the midst of all the protest and confrontation concerning the structures of the Church, there is no trace of it in the Movement? It almost seems as if you are not interested in these problems, but concerned only with maintaining your fidelity to the Church and obeying the directives of the Holy Father and the Hierarchy. Do you really feel that you can ignore the reasons which are at the basis of the protest movement?

Fr. Silvano: After all I told you, are you sure you still need an answer? Well okay, I'll answer with a slogan that we have adopted from the Gen. "If we want to change anything, we have to start with ourselves." It is not a change in structures that changes our lives. At best, it can make it easier. You can be sure, however, that wherever there is a new life, the old structures certainly change.

7. "NEW PARISHES":
REDISCOVERING THE COMMUNITY

During this series of interviews about the many different facets of the Focolare Movement on its 30th Anniversary, I went to visit the Center for the New Parish Movement situated just north of Grottaferrata near Rome. It is one of the most recent expressions of the Focolare spirituality. Father Joseph Arruano was on hand to answer my questions.

Everyone Co-responsible

Q.: On a recent visit to the Mariapolis Center in Rocca di Pappa, I came upon a large group of people, which in itself is nothing unusual, but this time the crowd was made up of many different kinds of people. There were young and old, entire families, engaged couples, blue-collar workers, executives, secretaries, sales women, carpenters, physicians, and so on. They were speaking many different languages, such as German, Spanish, Italian, and Yugoslavian. There were also several priests among them.

Out of curiosity I asked who they were. They told me that they were participating in a four-day meeting of the New Parish Movement. They explained to me that the priests among them were their pastors and that they had come from different European countries. Each pastor had with him some of his parishioners.

When I hear the word "pastor," I can't help thinking of the pastor of my town when I was a child. At least at that time, there was a sort of "paternalism" about pastors. I remember feeling that if I had asked my good-natured pastor, "Who are you?" he would not have answered, "I am a minister of God," but, "the minister of Almighty God." I don't know if I am explaining myself.

The pastors I saw that day at Rocca di Papa seemed to be quite different from my old image. They were being pastors among their people in the same simple way as any worker doing what he's called to do. I don't know why, perhaps because they didn't try to stand out from the others in any way. From that moment on, I was curious to know more about them, but I could tell that they were real leaders even if they didn't try to stand out from the others in any way. From that moment on, I was curious to know more about the New Parish Movement.

I took advantage of the occasion offered by this series of interviews to find out more about the New Parish Movement. Therefore, Father Joe, could you tell me something that would give me a concise view of this Movement?

Fr. Joe: So you are surprised by this new group of pastors. Yet it is normal now to see pastors, priests, and laymen form an authentic community so that the parish does not become a bureaucratic institution.

How did all this come about? For years now, we priests of the Priests' Branch have been living the spirituality of

Above: **Turin, Italy. St. Joan of Arc Parish** is one of the "new parishes." The Sunday Eucharistic Celebration is the moment in which the parishioners renew their unity. The parish, like many others where the Focolare spirituality is lived, is a center of attraction for many.
Below: A real family life results from living the new commandment in the parish.

Above: **Brazil. Some young people of a parish community** with their pastor in the State of Paraná. The girl near the pastor had been elected "Miss Paraná." After having encountered this community, she decided to commit herself to a Christian life without compromise.
Below: Parishioners of a "New Parish" in Germany.

the Focolare Movement. We found in it the evangelical meaning of a communitarian life. Little by little, our life of unity grew in intensity and began to involve other persons who were interested in this same experience. We understood then that if this spirit could be brought to the members of the parish community, we would be able to give the parish a new look. The parishioners, too, would rediscover their place in the local Church.

On the other hand, we had before us some pretty significant facts. We had noticed, for instance, that the members of the Focolare Movement, once they had begun to live the adventure of Christian love, spontaneously turned more frequently to the sacraments. They participated more actively in the life of the Church. Mutual love, which is the essence of our Christian life, always leads to a community-oriented spirit. We priests and the lay people live our community life in the parish. The parish is the small piece of the Church where God wants us to live our Christianity day after day. In a few words, we felt we had found the "precious pearl of great price," that is the possibility of being a community and therefore a real parish. We began sharing in a relationship which was both human and divine, and experiencing a special presence of Jesus renewing the souls of the faithful and enlightening every aspect of the life of the community. The spirituality of the New Parish Movement is precisely the spirituality of the Focolare Movement lived in the context of the local Church.

In April 1967, for the first time, a few groups of

parishioners and their pastors were invited to a meeting at the Mariapolis Center in Rocca di Papa. For three days we lived together and practiced living as a family. The people in the Focolare Movement shared their experiences with us.

The parishioners, on their return to the parishes, while remaining in their associations or groups, began with their pastors to live what they had experienced in Rocca di Papa at the service of the parish. They discovered in different ways that this evangelical life, lived by all together, was just what the parish needed.

Within their parishes, the people are united with one another and to their pastors, and consider themselves to be co-responsible for the entire spiritual and social life of the parish. They are Christians who, in giving of themselves, have found the joy, as Pope Paul VI would say, "of being Christians."

Presently, there are not too many such communities in the world, even though their number is growing constantly. They are scattered all over Europe, in nations such as Germany, Italy, Austria, Switzerland, Belgium and Spain. Outside of Europe, we find them in Brazil, Argentina, and also in Korea. Some of these communities are made up of hundreds of people, others are smaller, but all live the same spirit and experience.

A New Sense of Fraternity

Q.: If I have understood correctly, the New Parish

Movement is made up of parish communities which, as you mentioned, have experienced a new blossoming because of an authentic evangelical life. This is all very interesting, since it comes at a moment when, on all sides, we hear about the failure of this traditional institution, the parish. It is one crisis among many, but it does exist, however, and it has to be faced. I would like to ask you, therefore, what is the strategy, or better, to use a more appropriate term, what are the pastoral guidelines which guarantee this new blossoming in the parishes?

Fr. Joe: In order to do away with any misunderstandings, let me say something right away. We have never tried to sit down at a conference table and work out any projects, nor did we set down any pastoral guidelines. As you know, as soon as a priest becomes a pastor, he usually begins making projects. We change and change, we organize and reorganize, yet nothing ever happens. What I mean is that the people are always the same, each with his own individual problem, standing shoulder to shoulder with one another, and yet never entering into a true communion. What kind of a parish is that? Something has gone wrong somewhere.

We believe that we have found what went wrong. We had simply forgotten that each neighbor is Jesus and that, in his presence, not even the pastor can set himself above the others as teacher and judge without first acknowledging his neighbor as a brother, since we are all called to live the same evangelical experience, even though in different roles. Before God, it is not important whether we are men or women, rich or poor, Jew or Greek, nor does it matter whether we are priest or laymen; am I clear?

This has had many consequences. Let me tell you right away that there is nothing extraordinary about us. We are ordinary people and far from perfect. You will find in our communities the same kind of people that exist in any social group. There is a difference, however. In our relationship with one another, before everything else, before thinking about organizations, programs, liturgical celebrations and so on, we try to love one another. We try to serve our brother, to understand him beyond all differences of age, culture, social class, personal defects or limitations, and so on. Little by little, we have seen that a new sense of fraternity was born among us and that we were becoming more and more a family, one body.

I can assure you that wherever this life is being lived, it brings about a real evangelical revolution. These communities have something of the beauty of the early Christians. They are communities where in the midst of everyday life, a continous testimony is offered to God.

No Discrimination or Narrow-mindedness

Q.: I agree, and I think we have seen clearly that today's parish is no longer confined to the parish church or to the priests' residence, but that it is a living body in which the priest is one among the others, even though he has a specific task to fulfill. However, there is still a doubt in my mind. The term "parish" is often synonymous with a closed entity, a self-contained world that is alive and vital within its own boundaries, but it does not go beyond itself.

Fr. Joe: There is no denying that this problem does exist. Every group tends to be closed within itself. However, when a group shares in the goal of the Focolare Movement, which is one of working toward the fulfillment of Jesus' prayer "That all may be one," there is no room for discrimination or narrow-mindedness. The bachelor and the married man, the student and the farmer, the executive and the laborer, the young and old are one anothers neighbors. All must live the same Gospel together. The young man involved in the C.Y.O., the Jesuit priest, the non-Catholic neighbor − all are called, as Christians, to give their lives for one another and to be members of one body.

On the other hand, our experience has shown us that we grow both individually and collectively inasmuch as we share our lives. Thus, if parishes were closed within themselves, they would certainly die out. We need to communicate our life to others, since it is in giving and not in receiving, that we grow.

I believe that even this need for communion among parishes is typically evangelical. (It was the same for the early Christian communities.) The meetings that we hold periodically so that the parish communities from different regions and different nations might get together are a confirmation of this. There you can hear many different people talk about their experiences which are prompted by charity and which encompass the different aspects of the life in the parish. They include the communion of goods, the apostolate, spiritual life and prayer, the works of mercy, hospitality, mass media, and so on.

In Germany, inter-parochial relationships exist also between Catholic and Lutheran parishes. They share the experiences of a life based on the Gospel.

There are other factors which show concretely that these communities consider themselves as one family. They have a new way of looking at their own finances and at the administration of their own goods. There are parishes where the people may sacrifice some necessary items from their own households in order to provide for the more urgent needs of other communities. For example, a group of German parishes send their suplus every month to Brazil to help the parish communities of Palmares in the Northeast. This is not done as a missionary offering, but as a natural sharing of goods among the members of the same church community. This surplus that they share is the fruit of personal sacrifice and of careful family budgeting, focused not on the particular needs of the family itself but on the needs of the entire community.

Unity Is Not Uniformity

Q.: From what you have said, I can see that we are dealing with parishes in Europe, America, and also in Asia. In other words, you are speaking of parishes situated in different environments. Don't you think that there is a danger of the "New Parish Movement" trying to create an elite group where uniformity prevails?

Fr. Joe: As I mentioned, we have no fixed patterns or programs to be followed during a particular month or year. First of all, it could never be possible since these New Parishes are scattered all over the world. We follow, however, our own line. Pastors and congregations want to make the Gospel part of their lives, and to serve one another according to the choice that each one has freely made. There are meetings, which could give the idea of a certain form of organization (and it may also be true if we agree on the meaning of the term), but they are a precious opportunity to help us discover new dimensions for our own spiritual life as well as for our communitarian and social commitment. As for the rest, each community with its determining human factors, geographic location, and type of culture will then discover in living the Gospel those distinctive features which are proper to it. It is living the Gospel that unifies, and not some kind of cultural uniformity, don't you agree?

There are some New Parishes in a poor region of Brazil. In this region, many believe that it is impossible to bring the message of the Gospel unless you first bring about social progress. We have seen, however, that there is social progress in the measure in which the members of the parish community live this Christian experience. For instance, the meaning of family unity and a desire to study in order to overcome illiteracy has come alive in them. If they must move elsewhere because of work, their newly acquired sense of stability helps them adjust to a new environment without trauma. They take an active part in the life of the new community to which they now belong.

In other words, what is important is that everything that develops should be "life." Life is not a cliché, however, but something that organizes itself according to its needs and requirements.

What is beautiful is that, once we discover that we are all brothers, we can share this life. Even if it is quite different for each, it still originates from the same source. We then feel enriched by one another. It seems that we no longer belong to one particular country or another, because we participate in the same life everywhere. We go, as the Gen would say, from being European or African or American to becoming the "World-Man."

The Particular Which is Universal

Q.: You have shown me a very positive picture. At the same time, however, it arouses a suspicion within me. Don't you think that the New Parish Movement, born within and nurtured by the spirituality of the Focolare Movement, might risk confining parishioners to a specific formula, namely, the Focolare formula, which without a doubt is very beautiful and interesting, but is still only a particular one?

Fr. Joe: Of course, people cannot be forced into a particular experience. If we tried to do this, the community would automatically be divided and this would be contrary to the very nature of the experience which aims at making the parishioners one among themselves. If it is true that the Focolare Movement, from which the New Parish Movement has received its inspiration, is only a detail in the Church, it is also true (as has been stated by the other people you have interviewed, that its spirituality is universal because it is the Gospel.

The Franciscan Order is also a detail, a paricular, but the spirit of poverty reenkindled by it is an evangelical requirement for everyone who wishes to follow Christ. In other words, not everybody is called to enter the Franciscans, but anyone who wants to be a Christian must live poverty in one way or another. What is it that God wants of the Focolare Movement? That, by its testimony, true love among men, among families, among nations be enkindled. What is it that we of the New Parish Movement desire? That all the members of a parish community live the commandment to love one another, not in words but in deeds. Does this mean we want to "Focolarinize" them? No. We just wish to help everyone to be more Christian.

Rediscovering the Mystery of the Eucharist

Q.: Many of the old values seem to be irreparably lost. They are no longer appreciated. It seems that even the parish as such, with all its organizations, doesn't hold any interest for men. Add to this what someone has told me, "while the man of today is crushed by economic, social and political problems and finds it increasingly difficult to find God, the parishes seem merely to offer services for some of the traditional, and by now bureaucratic, practices." What does the New Parish Movement have to offer in a situation like this?

Fr. Joe: I like this question. Actually I've been waiting for it. I would say that the parish is not so much a place where men build their own house in order to live religion together. Rather, it is the presence, the truly alive presence, of Another who sets up his dwelling among men. It is He who comes to live in their midst to help them, to sustain them in their difficulties, to enlighten them in the solutions to their problems, to become their companion, to reunite them day by day in that unity of which the Trinitarian family is the model and goal to be reached. When two or three, or twenty, are united in his love, then also simple things like talking, sports, taking a walk, working, or resting become ways to live the entire day with Jesus present among us.

If we do not live in this way, all the things we do, even the most praiseworthy ones, have little value for the kingdom of heaven. On the other hand, the more we live the "where two or three. . ." of the Gospel, the more everything becomes an expression of the supernatural, a manifestation of the divine in human activities.

This experience brings about substantial results. We realize it every time we hear statements like these, which we hear rather often: "Yes, now I do believe that God exists and that He is Love. For one can almost feel His presence in your midst." Other times people said their ideas were clarified, as recently happened to a theology student who told us: "For some time, I have asked myself if it was true that Jesus is still alive. Then I met a community living united in the name of Jesus, and I said to myself, 'He is truly present there.' I have found the answer to my doubts. It was logical then for me to think that if Jesus is alive today, certainly he must have existed 2,000 years ago and therefore what the Gospel says is true. Now I understand the Eucharist, the Church, the sacraments, and also authority in an entirely different way. I can also say that when a community accepts Jesus, he dwells there and the parishioners become his members, his Body. I have found the Church."

I could go on telling you about the many instances where people's lives have changed, about the gifts of light and new understanding which many have received.

People who have come in contact with this reality are taken by it. Traditional practices, which are not accepted today because they no longer hold any meaning, acquire renewed life in the light of this new spirit. The liturgy is coming to life again. This is certainly not a result of exterior innovations brought about by reform nor by particular external things. It is due to the fact that the members of the community acquire a new understanding of the Eucharistic celebration. They understand the significance of making the Eucharistic mystery the center of their lives. Many who do not belong to the community feel attracted to the parish. We have heard them say many times that "in coming to Mass in your church, I have found

God," or, "You are a real community," and "Your Mass gives me the strength for the entire week."

This is our experience, and if this reality penetrates into the parish, then the structures and valid practices which belong to the Gospel will remain. But those structures and practices which have come about during certain historical periods and are already outdated will disappear. Jesus in the midst of his own people, as it has been said, passes "like a fire that consumes all that must fall and leaves standing only the truth." In the face of a secularized world and a spreading hedonistic vision of life, of the dechristianization of Catholics and the disunity among priests which causes disunity among the faithful, we feel that we have rediscovered a simple way to obtain results which seemed to us unattainable. Our limitations and shortcomings remain. The answer, however, lies in establishing living communities made up of Christians — as Paul VI would say — who are bound together by mutual love and thus able to generate the presence of Christ in their midst. And believe me, this is some program!

8. A CHARISM FOR UNITY

This time, our interview concerns the religious connected with the Focolare Movement. Representatives of five different religious orders were present. They were Father Andrew Balbo, O.F.M., from the Vatican Secretariat for Non-Believers; Father Joseph Savastano, Vicar General of the Society of the Catholic Apostolate; Father Santino Bisignano, Superior of a Seminary of the Oblates of Mary Immaculate; Father Angelo Lazzarotto, Assistant General of P.I.M.E., and Father Paul Bachelet, a Jesuit who is Dean of the Regional Seminary at Anagni. These priests were a small representation of a far wider group of religious from many congregations who know and live the spirituality of the Focolare Movement.

More Than Eighty Religious Families

Q.: Not long ago, as I happened to pass by that busy place which is the Mariapolis Center in Rocca di Papa, I saw there about 125 religious of many different orders and congregations. They had come from every part of Western Europe, and some, I think, even from Eastern Europe. I was told that they were having a meeting of the National Secretariats of the Religious connected with the Focolare Movement. "I see," I told myself at first. On second thought, I realized that I didn't really see or understand much except for one thing, namely, that the religious do not have, as do the priests, their own movement inspired by the Focolare ideal. I asked Father Balbo, what then are these National Secretariats which exist not only in Europe, but in other continents as well. I was curious to know how many religious of different orders, institutes, or congregations belong to them, and if there were cloistered monks among them.

Fr. Balbo: From time to time, we religious also come to the Mariapolis Center at Rocca di Papa for our meetings. Our presence there shows another aspect among the many which give life to the spirituality of the Focolare Movement.

I'm not surprised to hear you say that, in a way, you understand who we are, and yet you don't quite understand us. The people you have interviewed so far, in fact, represent groups that are substantially homogeneous, and also much larger in size. You could, therefore, easily grasp how the spirituality of the Movement is reflected both in the individual, as well as in the whole. With the religious, on the other hand, the personal relationship is, in a way, absorbed in a wider and far more complex reality. Each one of them, in fact, represents a world defined by and imbued with a different charism. By charism, I mean a particular way of life with its own specific spirituality and structure, a life that is dictated by the inspiration of the founder and by the rule which puts it into a concrete form.

Thus, our story is more delicate and interesting. In fact, we must receive the contribution offered to us by the spirituality of the Movement in the framework of the divine plan which, in the words of Vatican II, unfolds itself in the "marvelous variety of religious communities" which came into being through the action of the Holy Spirit and are approved by the Church "for the edification of the body of Christ" and for the "manifestation of the manifold wisdom of God."

Each one of us, as a religious, is already part of a body that has its own characteristics, its own spirituality and structure. Therefore, for a religious, there is not, nor can there be any movement like the Priests' Movement which is juridically bound to the Focolare Movement.

The Focolare spirituality has spread widely in the different religious families through its spontaneous acceptance by the members. It is truly amazing to see how this is reflected in the differnt orders and in each according to its particular nature.

The extent to which it has spread is shown by the fact that at the Convention of Rocca di Papa 125 religious from several European countries were present. They represent about 60 different orders and congregations. This picture is only a partial one, however. For in addition to the meetings at the Mariapolis Center, there are also meetings which are held regularly in different countries of the world. Furthermore, it would be interesting to mention the influence of the spirituality of the Movement among the missionaries, and how it has spread through them in the countries where they are, particularly in Africa and Asia.

Although we have never attempted to compile any statistics, the number of religious I am speaking of amounts to several thousand, belonging to more than 80 religious families. Some are contemplatives and others are in active life. Some belong to the most ancient orders, and others to the most recent congregations and institutes. Meetings, such as the one you mentioned, are attended by priests and brothers, holding different positions and belonging to different generations, in an atmosphere of great brotherly love.

In this context, it will be easier to understand what the function of the National Secretariats is. Their task is to give all religious the opportunity to get to know the spirit of the Focolare Movement in a way that is suited to their state of consecration. They promote a deepening of the spirituality of each individual order in an evangelical spirit of unity. It is done in such a way as to help each order preserve and enhance its own characteristic features and its own function.

The secretariats are made up of religious who have been appointed by their superiors or who have had permission to work there. They are chosen from among those who have had long experience in the life of the Focolare Movement. It goes without saying that their superiors can give them a different assignment at any moment, because they retain full authority over them. The position of these religious involved in the work of the secretariat is no different from that of any of their brothers in their orders or congregations. Besides this, all religious ask for their superior's permission each time they are called to participate in a meeting for them at the Mariapolis Center or elsewhere.

Isn't Your Rule Enough for You?

Q.: In the light of the jealous, I would almost say exclusive, chauvinistic attitude I have often noticed among the members of a particular order towards all other religious orders, I must say that this is really extraordinary news. You are speaking of religious from 80 different orders getting along beautifully, in peace and harmony. Tell me, Father Savastano, what is it that keeps you together?

Fr. Savastano: In regard to the chauvinism you speak of, I don't expect to convince you of the contrary, but I would like you to consider a very important element concerning religious orders and congregations. At the basis of every one of them, there is a reality as you know, a reality for which every member has left everything and which constitutes his new being. You can understand, therefore, their attitude, without, of course, any of its exaggerated forms, when it comes to defining an identity, a reality which comes from God. Men will pass away, but that reality will remain forever.

Going back to your question, however, I would like to answer it by telling you something about our experience.

As you know, quite a few religious have had the opportunity of being in touch with the Focolare Movement since its beginning, first in Trent in 1943, then in Rome in 1947, and later on wherever the Movement spread. In many different countries, these religious actually shared the Movement's growing pains. Furthermore, they were very often the ones who spread the spirituality of the Focolare wherever they would go on their travels.

The contact with the first Focolarini and their experiences based on the Gospel and on unity, were so genuine and so original that they found a very special echo in the hearts of these religious, suggesting a dimension of life more in tune with the spirit of the Church, a fresher and more immediate approach to their own religious consecration. I would like to mention that these were the years in which religious communities were beginning to feel the effects of the new vision brought about by the encyclical *Mystici Corporis*. About this time, a group of twelve religious from different Institutes went to see Father Larraona, who was secretary of the Congregation for Religious. They talked to him about the effects that the spirituality of the Movement was having in different environments, and of the group which had sprung from it.

To give you an idea of what happened to us, I would like to remind you of what happened to the whole Church at the time of St. Francis. All Christians had to look into their own lives in the light of the Saint's new message of love and poverty.

We, too, were greatly attracted and challenged by this

Above: **Religious** belonging to more than eighty orders and congregations, through their contact with the Focolare spirituality, deepen their individual spirituality in an evangelical spirit of unity. This helps them, in many cases, to rediscover the charism of their founders. The unity among religious of different orders helps each order to preserve and enhance its own characteristic features and its own function in the Church.

Below: **Religious** from different countries participating in an international summer course on the spirituality of the Focolare.

Going to God Together

Jesus demands that our love be communal, not only a personal love for God, not only a personal love for our neighbor; for our love cannot reach its fullness, cannot attain its completion until it becomes reciprocal.

Jesus does not say that it is sufficient simply to love one's neighbor. Rather he says, "Love one another as I have loved you." He wants reciprocal love to be a fundamental aspect of our Christian life. And this is also part of the mystery of going to God together. We cannot go to God alone. Unless our love is reciprocal, it is not that perfect Christian love which God asks of us.

Pascal Foresi
(from *Reaching For More*)

new charism. The life of this new community which was being formed reminded us again of the words of the Gospel. It gave us a new understanding of how to live the Priestly Prayer of Jesus, "That all may be one." The meeting with this spirituality left a deep imprint on our personal lives. We were perfectly aware of the questions that were being put to us from all sides, "Isn't your rule enough for you? What else is there for you to learn, and so on?"

In the beginning, our experiences were confined to a personal level, even though many religious actively participated in the summer Mariapolis. As the Movement grew and began to form itself into its different expressions (the Focolarine and the Focolarini, the married Focolarini, the volunteers, and so on), we realized that we did not fit in any of these categories. At this point, we spontaneously began to meet among ourselves, first in Rome and then in other cities as well. It was the beginning of a real experience of unity among religious.

During these meetings, we tried to assimilate and to live the different aspects of the Focolare spirituality. We discovered then that we were forming one family. The characteristics of each member of it, however, were well defined and strengthened The sharing, in fact, made each of us possess the patrimony of the Church which was contained in every religious order. Every time we met together, we felt we had to convert all over again so that we could be genuine in our vocation. We became more and more aware of the fact that we could not possess the spirit of the Church without having a strong bond with one another, and fully living the life of the Mystical Body. For two or twenty or eighty orders and congregations that are alive and in step with the Church form a single harmony.

Relationships Change

Q.: What happens in a religious community when one or more of its members adopt this new spirit which gives a completely new dimension to the rule, the vows, to all the concrete expressions of each individual spirituality? I'm asking this, Father Bachelet, because I know full well that at times it takes just a trifle to disturb the life of a religious community, especially if this trifle is something new and the community life is routine.

Fr. Bachelet: We would like, first of all, to bear witness to this new spirit by living it without disturbing the community with a lot of talk. We must admit, however, that the desire of sharing the gift that we have received has at times led us to exaggeration, and this did cause disturbance. You want to know, I believe, what really happens when a few members of a community come to know the Movement's spirituality. The answer is that relationships begin to change.

For example, one of the most controversial aspects of religious life today is obedience. Wherever the spirit of unity enters a community, it not only helps overcome the controversy, but establishes a rapport of love between the superior and the subject, and obedience is the fruit of this mutual love. In this new dimension, relationships develop to such perfection that there is unity of mind and heart. All the other aspects of community life (the vows, the rule, the schedule, and so on), which might appear negative, acquire a new perspective; they become signs of communion, functional instruments which help everyone to live the perfection of charity in the present moment.

Of course, situations vary from order to order. Among the 80 or so orders and congregations that we are talking about, there are some in which only a few of the members live the spirituality of the Movement. There are others where there is a whole group, and still others where the entire community or province lives the spirituality. Moreover, in some cases the spirituality of unity is adopted by an institute as a whole.

A Look at Our Founders

Q.: We all know, Father Lazzarotto, that religious life of the traditional orders, with their rules, obedience, etc., is not in good standing today, especially with young people. They consider religious life outmoded, bound to conditions and to social structures which are long dead and buried. Even those who show a more favorable attitude still think that that kind of life is far from the best or most valid way of living their faith today. Is it still possible, in spite of all this, to speak of religious life as of something modern and fitting our times?

Fr. Lazzarotto: We certainly do feel modern and timely. These twenty years that we have been in contact with the Movement have been a school of "aggiornamento." When the ideal of the Focolarini was born in 1943, it was nothing but a rediscovery of the Gospel in order to live out the choice of God in a way that would go with the times. Well, in one way or another, the same phenomenon occurred at the beginning of the different religious families. In other words, the religious families were born as an answer to the needs of mankind at a particular time. The different founders, enlightened by God, found in the evangelical life, the necessary strength and the light to give the answer needed in their specific historical period. Obviously, they expressed themselves with works and structures which were then quite timely and appropriate for a life based on the Gospel. With the changing of times and the conditions of human life, the forms adopted by the various founders can change, but the basic reality of an evangelical life remains and is always modern. If the founders of the different religious orders were alive today, they would express their individual charisms in the light of today's needs. This means that they would live the Gospel in a form that is up-to-date and modern. This is precisely what the spirituality of the Focolare Movement helps us to accomplish, that is, it helps us to be more authentic in our respective vocations. It helps us to understand how we can be what our founders would be today. The Gospel is always modern. We have also seen that the man of today *is* attracted to religious life if it is truly based on the Gospel.

If religious families stray from the Gospel, it is because their founders have not been correctly interpreted and the members have focused their attention mostly on the external aspects of their life, instead of being, as they were, a living Gospel.

Also Vatican II, in giving the guidelines for the renewal of religious life and its adaptation to our time, has proposed as the supreme rule the following of Christ as taught in the Gospel and a return to the original inspiration of the founders. This was the best confirmation of the experience we had made in these past years in living the spirituality of the Movement. It has been, in fact, an experience of an interior renewal, according to the original inspiration that God had given to our religious families, of overcoming differences in particulars in order to go to the essential, and in so doing to reach out to modern man. All of this has been done with the strength that comes from unity and communion with the other orders.

Once a communion of mutual love among the different religious orders is established, each order is enriched by the light and experience of the others. Therefore, our motto is, "Let us love the order of the other as our own." Unity and enrichment, not a new structure, are the fruits of the spirituality of the Movement among religious.

An Antidote for the Crisis

Q.: You must admit, Father Bisignano, that in recent years, the religious orders have been touched by a profound

and almost overwhelming crisis. The abandonment of mon-
asteries and convents and the emptying out of seminaries
are the most evident signs of this phenomenon. Do you
think that this new spirit can offer an antidote for this
crisis in religious orders, and bring about new vocations?

Fr. Bisignano: At the time the Movement came into
being during the last World War, the crisis which is now
existing in the Chruch, and in humanity as a whole, was far
from showing any signs. The spirituality of the Movement,
this charism of unity, was a gift, a remedy prepared and set
by God as an answer to the needs, ills, and problems of
today. Therefore, those of us who were living this evangelical life based on unity were spared the crisis which
exploded later on. Of course, we had our share of suffering
because of it, but it seemed that by the time the crisis
came, in one way or another, we had already overcome it.
As we witnessed what was happening in the different
religious orders — defections, lack of vocations, questioning
of the value of vows, and so on, we felt that we were
already living the solution. We went ahead and experienced
a blossoming of life which enabled us to help the others.

On the other hand, this crisis, though deeply painful, did
not seem to be entirely negative, in the sense that it
oriented us toward what is essential, authentic, and permanent.

The fact that religious orders suffer the same crisis that
plagues all of mankind only shows how deeply they are
rooted in humanity itself. Just as single parts of humanity
react in different ways when it comes to reexamining

human structures, religious orders feel that they too should change certain forms in their structures which hinder the return to the simplicity and authenticity of their life. In this way, everything that is not genuine collapses.

If in considering the crisis, we limit ourselves to consider the empty seminaries and the number of defections, we would only be skimming the surface. The experience of these years has confirmed that, together with the crisis, there has also been a deepening of religious life and a greater commitment to living it in an authentic way. This has occurred not by breaking down and doing away with the structures, nor by creating new ones, but by giving greater value to the heritage left us by our founders and by the Church. The existence of the Secretariat that you asked about is a confirmation that this is so. A new life, without the need for particular new structures, blossomed. It is a life where nothing that is valid in the different congregations is denied or left aside. On the contrary, it is enhanced by a new dimension which is the fruit of the experience of unity. This experience has taken place not within a specific religious family, but among the different religious families as well (this is what is extremely new), and the number of religious who have chosen this life is constantly growing. Their superiors are happy about the contact they have with the Movement. There is also an increase in the number of religious participating in the meetings all over the world.

The majority, or at least a good part of the religious, are young. For it is the young religious who show the greatest concern for authenticity. Their presence helps all of us to be so. There is no gap or break between the two gene-rations. As for the vocations, I must add that something quite amazing is happening. Many young people, when they first get to know this life, either at the meetings organized by the secretariats, or from contact with a religious com-munity where the spirit is lived, feel drawn to it; they feel the call to live in the same way. Often they are young people who have qualifications for a good career; they have degrees and professional training, yet they choose life in a monastery. In addition to what I have seen in our own theological student bodies and in our youth groups, I have found other confirmations of this fact during recent visits throughout Europe. Perhaps, it is still only a seed, but we know that it is the prelude to a new blossoming.

To conclude, I would like to add that the number of religious who are united in the spirit of the Movement and who relive today the charism of their founders with freshness and authenticity, shows how the charism of the Focolare Movement is truly like Mary in its service of other charisms.

9. WOMEN RELIGIOUS

At the International Secretariat for Women Religious connected with the Focolare Movement, we met Sister Immaculata, Vicar General of the Sisters of Mary, from Ingelmunster, Belgium. Sister is one of the persons responsible for the Secretariat. We asked Sister some questions which might be of interest to our readers.

Q.: I recall that during a general audience on April 14, 1971, Paul VI offered some words of encouragement and blessing to a group of sisters from different orders and congregations "associated with the Focolare Movement," as he called them. This gave me the idea that a real Movement for religious inspired by the spirit of the Focolare existed. If this is so, Sister, how and where did it begin? Are there many congregations and orders that are open to this spirituality?

Sr. Immaculata: The words of the Holy Father on that occasion were, as we understood them, "And now, another large group. They are religious coming from many countries. They are associated with the Focolare Movement. . . . We bless all of you from our heart, your individual religious families and, above all, we bless your resolution to bring into your congregations the ardent flame of love and of the charity of Christ."

You asked me when this life began among sisters. We

were present in the Movement since its very beginning in 1943-44. At times, it was the sisters who, by their testimony, were the instruments of God for the spreading of this spirit in their own congregations, in schools, and in hospitals in many different countries. This happened in the missions as well and, therefore, in very far away countries. It would be difficult to give you any statistics about our numbers. We are very many, so many as to make up a real body of consecrated people who have renewed their lives, even in the silence of their cloister.

Q.: How have you maintained and developed the bond that exists among you?

Sr. Immaculata: Every year, we meet in the Mariapolis. However, in order to deepen our experience of unity, other meetings are prepared especially for religious. I remember, for example, a meeting that took place in 1968 in Belgium with 500 sisters from many different congregations, countries, and even from the missions.

Sisters also meet regularly with the approval of their superiors wherever Focolare Centers exist in the world. As a result of these meetings, the need for a permanent International Secretariat for Women Religious who are part of the Focolare Movement came into being at the Mariapolis Center in Rocca di Papa.

Meetings for postulants, junior sisters, and novices from different congregations are held. An international meeting is held every year for those sisters who are responsible for this unique branch of the Focolare Movement. During a general audience with the Holy Father, they received further encouragement and his special blessing.

Q.: What are the effects of the contact with this spirituality?

Sr. Immaculata: I would like to say that before everything else, this contact with the Movement helps us to live out our vocation in a radical way, to focus on the essential values of our life, that is, our personal relationship of love with Christ, the cross, Mary, prayer, the vows, authority, and so on. We penetrate more deeply the charism of our founders in order to relive them today.

Another effect which I believe is the result of our contact with this spirituality is that of giving the different congregations the dimension of the whole Church and of humanity, and it has created among all of them a deep bond of unity. It is a bond that is based on God. As a result, many religious experience that before anything else, they are one family, the Church. Each congregation, then, has its own characteristics which are enhanced by this contact with other religious families.

As far as their relationship with the Focolare Movement is concerned, these sisters have a love for all the vocations and all the branches of the Movement which they try to help wherever they are. They also receive from these branches a precious contribution for their own works: the Gen Movement helps bring about a truly evangelical education in schools; the New Humanity Movement provides skilled experience in different fields of work; the New Family Movement gives a new insight in the assistance of families, orphans, and the aged; books and magazines furnish the material for religious formation, and so on.

In order to answer your question, I would say that this life of unity has brought about a real renewal in religious communities. If we are united in mutual love, Jesus is spiritually present among us and we are truly his followers. We have the light and strength to see and face the problems, sufferings, and difficulties that exist in every order or congregation. We are able to face them with an attitude of love, understanding, and mercy. Also, in this atmosphere of mutual love, the gap between generations disappears because love knows no age.

Finally, this life of unity helps us to be more faithful to our vocation, and to renew our consecration to God even more radically and profoundly than the first time we gave ourselves to him.

Sisters belonging to different congregations and from different nations during a convention at the International Mariapolis Center in Rome.

10. NEW FAMILIES

> *Danilo and Anna Maria Zanzucchi live in a relatively new part of Rome not far from the wide, tree-shaded Nomentana Avenue. Danilo is an engineer. His wife is a pharmacist. Their five children are all in school. On the day of my visit to the Zanzucchis, I met another couple, Pino and Mariele Quartana, who are teachers.*
>
> *These two couples work at the World Center for the New Family Movement.*

The "New Commandment" Within the Family

Q.: When we consider the different movements of family groups having at their basis a conjugal spirituality, we wonder what is the specific characteristic of the New Family Movement that distinguishes it from the others.

Anna Maria: Expressions like "conjugal spirituality" and "family organization" are somehow foreign to us and do not fit in with our experience. You see, the New Family Movement is not a movement by itself, nor is it based specifically on a conjugal spirituality. It is, rather, an offspring of the Focolare Movement, or better, it was born within the Movement and it is permeated with the same spirituality.

The Focolare Movement, which repeats today the invitation to a Christian way of life, offers to married people the opportunity of participating in a different "life" by trying to put into practice, within their own family environment, Jesus' commandment, "Love one another as I have loved you." Jesus' love for us is the measure of love for one another, which we strive for and never fully achieve.

Each one of us, whether husband, wife, father, mother, or child, has discovered the extraordinary possibility of rooting the affection that we have for one another in a love which has its inspiration and model in the love of God itself. There we find the strength to be always less self-centered and more aware of the needs and desires of those around us. The basis of the New Family Movement stands here. At its core are the people who have felt the attraction to a life based on this love and who have said their own sincere and personal "yes."

As you can see, there is nothing special about our families, nor are we perfect. What we try to do, however, is to silence our own ego in order to listen to the others, to help and serve them regardless of faults, personality clashes, difficulties, misunderstandings, and unavoidable disappointments. This we feel comes before our career, well-being, or comfort.

As you can well imagine, our outlook on life changes completely. As someone has said, "the smallest service we perform, the smallest gesture of love, each difficulty which has been overcome, or each suffering which has been alleviated becomes an expression of our love for Christ in our spouse or in our children." If you want to know which is our characteristic, you could say that it is the effort (keeping in mind that we are trying, which doesn't mean that we always succeed) to live the "new commandment" of the Gospel in our married life. We try, in other words, to go back to the original meaning of Christian marriage, which according to St. Paul is a reflection of that "great mystery" which is the union of Christ and his Church. We feel very strongly that Christian marriage has the prophetic value of announcing to the world that in loving one another, as the Council has suggested, a husband and wife bear testimony to the "mystery of love which the Lord has revealed by his death and resurrection."

Q.: I do not think our readers know when the New Family Movement started and how it developed within the Focolare Movement. And, while you are at it, perhaps you could also tell us something about how the New Family Movement is organized.

Pino: The New Family Movement began, so to say, when in reality it already existed. It may sound like a word game, but it is true. Married people, fathers and mothers with their families, and young engaged people, all of whom had chosen to live the Gospel in all its authenticity, have always been a part of the Focolare Movement from its beginning. As Igino Giordani (see page 58) explained, in addition to the single Focolarini, who live a life in common, there are the married ones living with their families. They are, in fact, and have always been the animators of the New Family Movement, which had its start in 1967.

What the married Focolarini had to offer to the troubled and anguished world of the family was the fruits of their twenty years of experience. We realized that this meant a new commitment to act not only on a personal level, but also collectively, as a family.

You also asked about our organization. I guess you could call it that, as long as we agree about the meaning of the word. Every form of life, no matter how spontaneous it is, always adopts a kind of order. In other words, it organizes itself. What is important is that it remains "life." There are, of course, activities, gatherings, meetings for families, and so on. As I mentioned before, however, what matters most is the "life" within the families. The members of the New Family Movement get together not only to gain insight into their problems or to organize a particular apostolate, but above all to help one another live according to the "choice" each one has made and to be "carriers" of the Gospel's message with their lives.

I am sure you know that in the Focolare Movement we try to live a phrase of the Gospel which is chosen periodically and to which we try to conform our lives in order to "reevangelize" ourselves. In the New Family gatherings we try to better understand these words of the Gospel by living them and applying them especially to our family life. We then share the results of our efforts, our discoveries, our successes, and our difficulties. As you know, today's families are troubled and buffeted by all kinds of crises. What can be of great help to them is the friendship and understanding of other families. Frequently they need to be lifted out of their isolation which, in a great majority of cases, is the main cause of trauma and division in the family.

In a spontaneous sort of way, we arrived at a real sharing among us. It is not just an exchange of spiritual experiences, but a sharing at every level of life as well. For example, we share our time, our talents and capabilities, and whatever means we may have. In fact, we have reached the point where we can talk freely about our needs and, therefore, help one another materially as well as in other ways.

Don't think for a minute, however, that we are trying to form a sort of closed little group. If we did, life would die out. This kind of family life is open to all and shared with many others. To put it briefly, it is based on giving and not on receiving. We must always give, in order to be able to give always.

The social milieu around our families is imbued with a new life. The community in its simplest and most authentic form is, in a sense, reborn from its foundation up. I recently returned from a trip throughout Europe where I met with many groups of the New Family Movement. I also received letters from all over the world telling me about New Family gatherings, and even vacations spent together.

Families of Tomorrow

Q.: The old patriarchal family system has become some-

*thing of the past. The nuclear family which succeeded it is
already showing signs of disintegration. Some other possible
solutions have been suggested for the future, such as family
communities and so on. The experiments that have been
tried so far, however, have not been too successful. How
does the New Family Movement envision the family of
tomorrow?*

Danilo: What you have said about the patriarchal family
system is true, as far as the Western world is concerned. In
other parts of the world, the patriarchal family system is
still intact and it seems that some of its positive values are
becoming fashionable again; for example, respect for the
aged and having several generations living together in the
same dwelling.

Getting back to your question, however, we do not
believe that the family as an institution is dead. On the
contrary, groups of families working together can breathe
new life into the family system. If this has not happened
yet, it is because in some instances, we may have aimed at
the wrong goal. We may have focused on the community as
a cure-all that would liberate us from the suffocating four
walls of our home. We tried to substitute the family cell
with the group. As a result, the intrinsically right and just
desire not to be closed-in in our own little world sometimes
led to the dispersion of the family. Another consequence
was that it tended to create superficial and fragile relationships between husband and wife. We believe, however, that it
is precisely the unity between the spouses that must remain
intact; as the Scripture says, having left father and mother,

New Families Movement. Picnics are also an occasion for parents and children to deepen their unity in a relaxed atmosphere. *Above:* A picnic in New Jersey. *Below:* A picnic in the Chicago area.

The **"new commandment"** lived in the family creates a strong bond of unity between parents and children. All feel the responsibility to keep this unity growing, regardless of their age.

the two become "one flesh." In other words, we have to start with the family, and not with the group, in order to give new life to the community.

Things also work the other way around. Whenever I make an effort to establish more fraternal relationships with other families, I encounter sacrifices and have to overcome difficulties. All this, however, unites my wife, my family and me, for we go together through many and various experiences and accomplishments. There is no room in our life for monotony or boredom. On the contrary, we have a richer and more fulfilled family life. I can assure you that, in participating in the life of the Movement, the occasions for proving our availability are certainly not lacking. They are not lacking especially because we know that the commitment we made when we first started to live this life would lead us to prefer those families most marked by suffering and abandonment. We could say that our community, which spontaneously came into being, just as spontaneously took upon itself the burdens of many separations and traumas that have occurred in the lives of those families around us. We have tried to lighten the burden by helping couples to come together, by adopting orphaned, abandoned or handicapped children, by taking care of the elderly and the widowed, and by helping young drug addicts and ex-convicts to build a new life.

As far as the future of the family is concerned, we are not prophets. We do believe, however, that the answer is in the working together of families, where the spouses have, before everything else, a deep unity between them.

The Cure for a "Hidden Wound"

Q.: In an effort to save families from disintegration, some family groups have adopted preventive, psychological techniques or the services of marriage counselors. How do you feel about these techniques for preventing or resolving matrimonial crises; and specifically, how do you deal with that "hidden wound" called lack of communication?

Mariele: One of the reasons for the communication gap we hear so much of, I think, is that we are inclined to focus on ourselves and our own little world; that is, we tend to be selfish and egocentric. The awareness that this is something we all experience should help us to be free of judgment and prejudice. It should help us to remember that we are all in the same boat. We feel that we can cure this gap by first of all curing selfishness in ourselves. This means that we have to come out of our own world, and be aware of others. At times, it requires a great effort, but it is necessary in order to tear down the barriers, especially those within the family.

When both a husband and wife are able to forget themselves out of love for each other, and when they actually do it, then difficult family situations change completely and unity is reestablished. As a result, they experience a sense of joy, fullness, and peace, even in the midst of suffering. The Scriptures tell us that these gifts come from the presence of God. We read in fact that where charity and love abide, there is God. It is in moments such as these that the sacrament of marriage is truly fulfilled: God makes of two creatures one flesh. When we meet other people and they see the serenity that exists between us, they are inevitably attracted to us and want to know our secret. The words of the Gospel, "By this love you have for one another, everyone will know that you are my disciples," become a reality.

You might ask, "What can be done if a husband and a wife are not able to communicate, due perhaps to their personalities, upbringing, or natural shyness?" Or else, consider the case of one who cannot easily communicate his or her intimate feelings even to those who are dearest to him. We know from experience that the best thing to do is, first of all, to accept the acute suffering we feel. Then, rather than attack the fortress in which the other is barricaded, adopt an attitude of respect, patience, and understanding. Once the other person feels free and at ease, it will be easier for him to open up and express himself.

You also asked what we think about psychological techniques, marriage counselors, and so on. We know that they can be very useful. In fact, if psychology can give people the "push" they need to get out of themselves and get to know others, it accomplishes a very beneficial function.

We find the "push" that we need to take these steps in our choice to live as Christians and in the help of the community in which we live. We can say from experience that it is possible to live in this way when we are incorporated into Christ, when we participate in his love. We find in him the strength to begin over and over again.

Q.: Families have suffered the most from the split between the old and new generations. We see children, who after having been raised in the traditional faith, embrace atheism, or react to the moderate views of their parents by taking extreme stands; or else they put an end to family differences by leaving home. I would like to know what the New Family Movement is doing to resolve these crises? How do parents deal with the situation if a child simply does not want to live in the spiritual climate of a "new family?"

Anna Maria: Some of our families have also experienced this general atmosphere of unrest. There have been crises, divisions, and children leaving home. These experiences, although not in great numbers, have helped us to understand the grief of so many families and the extreme importance of always having the charity St. Paul speaks of when he says, "Love is patient and kind . . . it is always ready to excuse, to trust, to hope and to endure whatever comes."

The different crises served as a test of the choice that we had made. This choice has helped many parents go beyond their own fear of rebellion in order to understand the true needs of their children. We have tried, regardless of circumstances, to maintain a close relationship with our children and to respect their "soul searching" and their suffering. Furthermore, their rebellion served as the stimulus for a deep examination of conscience. We saw, for example, how many things parents ask of their children for the sake of conformity, custom, tradition, or even just habit, instead of aiming at what is essential. We had to ask ourselves, how often we were prompted by a love that was, inasmuch as possible, similar to the love that God has for us. We know that what He wants is for our good, but He is patient, and above all, his love leaves us free.

We can say, moreover, that by continually sharing our experiences, we have been able to see even in this phenomenon which, at times, was painfully reflected in our own families, the need to be more authentic. In fact, as is often the case in Christian life, suffering when it is accepted and borne joyfully brings a new maturity to all the members of the family. We know from the Gospel that suffering is not something to be ignored, but rather that it has a great redemptive value. Parents who have experienced these conflicts with their children have suffered a great deal. We all know, however, that in each suffering we should recognize an aspect of Jesus' suffering. Many, therefore, were able to accept it without despairing and, in this way, to overcome crises which seemed to have no remedy. There have been many children who had become agnostics but who later returned to their families and to the faith. Some have even gone on to consecrate their lives to God.

Another thing that has helped us to achieve a better understanding of our children has been the continuous contact with members of the Gen Movement, the second generation of the Focolare Movement. It was this contact with the Gen that created a more understanding attitude toward the needs and inner turmoil that young people are experiencing.

This brings me to your other question on how we handle the situation when our children simply do not want to share the spiritual commitment of the family. It seems to us that the children may rebel against our errors, but they can never rebel against real love.

If the "spiritual climate" you mentioned before is as it should be (and we try our best to make it so) the children do not feel uneasy. If they do, then we have to reexamine our own way of acting. The spirituality that we have chosen is a way of life, and should not result in any constraint as far as our children are concerned. The children should always feel invited to share this life of union with God and with one another, but they should also be left completely free. We do not ask for any guarantees from them. All we want is to be able to help them discover their way in life, that is, what God wants for them, and not what pleases us.

Engaged Couples

Q.: It is a well-known fact that difficulties which destine a marriage to failure often begin before the couple is even married. This is due, in part, to the lack of preparation of a young couple for marriage. Today, to prevent this danger, there are pre-marital courses dealing with many aspects of married life. This is already a step in the right direction and an improvement over the past, but I do not think that it is sufficiently effective. Does the New Family Movement have anything to offer in this regard?

Pino: We believe that the first preparation for marriage takes place within the family itself. Our children, who will be the fiancés of tomorrow, should learn at home what mutual love means; that is, what it means for a husband and a wife to be ready to make whatever sacrifice is necessary out of love for one another. If they grow up in this environment, they will naturally tend to build a similar one.

Aside from this aspect, the New Family Movement is constantly in touch with young engaged couples. The friends of our children, acquaintances, teachers, and priests often turn to us either to prepare themselves or to be helped to prepare others for marriage.

You asked what we have to offer these couples. We have a high regard for premarital courses, counselors, the work of physicians and psychologists; and, at times, we even suggest this help to the young people who need it. We also participate in activities of this kind when we are invited to do so. However, we feel that our greatest contribution, our specific contribution, is to share with these young people our experiences. Many young couples have asked to participate in our family life. They want to see with their own eyes what it is to deal with one another, with the children, and so on.

You know how often it happens that youth come into contact with married people, who, even though they are Christian, are worn out and discouraged. Or else, they meet couples who remain together for social convenience and who live a routine life where there is no warmth or harmony. We feel that young people who are about to get married should see how the family can and should be in all its simplicity and beauty: a place where love blossoms and becomes lasting love; where love acquires all the different nuances of affection and sacrifice, as well as joy and fullness. When young people see that this kind of love is not a superficial feeling, but a deep reality which implies a life based on the Gospel, they want to know our secret. They want to make it their own in order to walk the same path. They, too, are a part of the New Family Movement and they enrich it with their fresh and youthful contribution.

Love, blossoming in the hearts of young people who have learned how to give God the first place in their lives, gets a new dimension. It is not a selfish love, but a love which is always ready to give, to make a sacrifice for others, always open to the needs of humanity. Engaged couples observe married couples, often their own parents, and thus learn how to grow in their love by having Jesus in the midst.

The presence of an older person in the family can be a source of problems sometimes. Frequently, however, it is a profoundly constructive "presence" that can give a valid contribution of affection and education to the growth of the little ones.

Istanbul, May 1972. The Patriarch Athenagoras and Chiara Lubich. The Patriarch had a deep love for the Focolare Movement and its foundress. He often introduced himself as a "humble member" of the Focolare. He considered its spirituality fundamental for true ecumenism.

11. THE ECUMENICAL ACTIVITY

Chiara Lubich, during her first meeting in 1967 with Patriarch Athenagoras, said that "for many years we believed that the spirituality of the Movement was only for Catholics; but because of the strong stress that is placed on the life of the Scriptures, we later realized that it was for all Christians who live it in accordance with their beliefs and with what the Holy Spirit suggests to them."

The first activities were not planned. Individuals and, later, groups met spontaneously until 1960. At that time, due to the increasing number of contacts, more structured activities became necessary, especially in Germany, England, North America, Australia, and the Middle East. And now, several annual conventions take place at the International Center of the Focolare Movement in Rome, Italy.

"Centro Uno" (Center for Unity) is the ecumenical office of the Focolare Movement in Rome. It coordinates the various ecumenical activities of the Movement. It is in contact and collaborates with various ecumenical bodies presently existing in the world.

Ottmaring: Ecumenism of Life

In Ottmaring, near Augsburg in Germany, a group of Focolarini, together with a group of Lutherans of the "Bruderschaft vom gemeinsamen Leben" (Brotherhood of

Communal Life), have opened an "Ecumenical Center" which has received the approval of the ecclesiastical authorities of both groups.

"We understood immediately that it was not enough to pay each other visits and hold meetings together, but as we were linked by the same ideal of life, it was vitally important to build a center where we could witness to this life together." Talking to Dr. Dieter Fürst, a Lutheran pastor and member of the "Kreuzbruderschaft" (Brotherhood of the Cross), who now lives permanently with his family at the Lutheran-Catholic ecumenical center at Ottmaring, we soon noticed that the key to this experience in ecumenism is not discussion or talks but life. This is emphasized in the name of the center: "Oekumenisches Lebens-Zentrum" (Ecumenical Center of Life). In order to understand exactly what is meant by "life" and to appreciate the quiet effectiveness and influence of this kind of ecumenism, it is necessary to trace the origins of the Ottmaring center and to take a look at its daily activity and witness.

It was in 1965, when a group of Lutherans met the Focolare Movement, that the idea first arose of building an ecumenical village of Christians united by the Movement's spirit of unity. Dr. Fürst describes this first encounter: "As members of a Bruderschaft, when we met the Focolare Movement, we immediately recognized in the Focolarini the same Holy Spirit who inspired our Brotherhood. The aim of our Brotherhood has always been unity, and unity among all Christians. When we met the Focolarini, we felt that God was offering us a chance to fulfill this objective."

Dr. Fürst, with Klaus Hess and other Lutheran pastors, was one of the co-founders of the center at Ottmaring which was opened in June, 1968. He moved permanently with his family to the center which, at present, has a total population of a hundred people. This is his account: "Now at Ottmaring there are two Catholic groups living in community and two Lutheran groups, as well as families of both churches. The individual groups and families go to work and lead their own lives in a very normal way. We are firmly convinced, however, that God wants us constantly to deepen the unity between us. This spiritual communion is visibly expressed in community prayer every evening; in the weekly participation of everyone — both Catholics and Lutherans — at a Catholic Mass and Lutheran service; in meetings among ourselves and with the numerous groups of visitors; in our ecumenical work that we have to develop together and the witness which presupposes the unity between us. And yet, with all this, we avoid suffocating the particular characteristics of each group and preserve absolute faithfulness to our own churches."

This utter faithfulness to the leaders of the respective churches and the complete backing and approval which have been accorded to the center as a result, distinguish the Ottmaring experiment as being of real significance for the churches concerned and an example for ecumenism on a wider scale. It is not a head-on attempt to build up friendlier relations between the individuals involved. Everyone at Ottmaring has the realistic awareness that they belong to their respective churches, exactly as they are today, and it is for the unity of these that they are working. Occasional visitors to Ottmaring find this hard to accept. "Some maintain that our ecumenical action could be more progressive," Dieter Fürst explains, "for example, they are shocked that intercommunion does not take place." And yet, for the inhabitants of Ottmaring, it is this very faithfulness to their respective traditions while consolidating a common Christian life, that gives the center its solid foundation and makes it an authentic sign of hope for ecumenism.

On the Catholic side, the Ecumenical Center was inaugurated in the presence of Cardinal Bea, the then President of the Secretariat for the Union of Christians and the Roman Catholic Bishop of Augsburg. Ever since, the Center has been encouraged constantly by the Roman Catholic authorities. The same attitude has been true of the Lutheran church. "Right from the start," Dr. Fürst recalls, "we made our plans known to the representatives of our church, always meeting with great confidence and understanding. This has been expressed recently in a practical way in the form of financial help for the new conference center. We have kept up close contacts with the leaders of our church in Munich and Augsburg, and we have set up other activities in other parts of Germany. Since, in a special way, we want to be an integral part of the local church, we have close contacts with the nearest Lutheran parish where I am often invited to hold services."

As the center has developed, according to Dr. Fürst, so has its influence widened. "Many friends of ours told us they would like to move to Ottmaring, and they did. Homes were built and, in this way, the center grew. This intense

Ottmaring, Germany. The new auditorium (above) and the dorms (below) inaugurated on May 1st 1976 in the ecumenical village of Ottmaring where Lutheran and Catholic communities, including several families, live in a spirit of unity. The characteristic ecumenism suggested by the people of Ottmaring is the result of living the Gospel together.

Ottmaring, Germany. Dr. Johannes Hanselmann, Lutheran Bishop of Bavaria, and the Catholic Bishop Joseph Stimpfle of Augsburg together bless the new facilities of the Ecumenical Center.

Dr. Fürst, whom we interviewed, together with Dr. Rupprech (left), Lutheran Dean for the region of Augsburg, and the Catholic Bishop Klaus Hemmerle (right) of Aachen, Germany, at the inauguration of the Ecumenical Center in Ottmaring.

communion of life led us to develop activities outside the center itself, and that work has produced its results — so much so that we have had to start building a large meeting hall and accommodations for guests.

"Individuals and groups visit the center in great numbers without any advertising on our part. Visitors ask us all the time what they must do to be able to settle down here. One of the most significant recent visits has been that of a group of forty-five members of the Synod of the Lutheran Church of Bavaria who came together with Dr. Johannes Hanselmann, Bishop of the Bavarian Lutheran Church, to get to know the way of life and the activities of Ottmaring.

"But we feel that the model of Ottmaring is a form of ecumenical life that can be lived everywhere. We have seen that this is so at meetings which we hold for people who are interested in our experience, at Nuremberg for southern Germany, and at Dortmund for the north. These meetings have given rise to small groups scattered all over the country, continuing our life, spreading Ottmaring elsewhere."

The main aim of the Ecumenical Center, however, is not to impress but to build unity through the ordinary day-to-day Christian life of its members. As Dr. Fürst frankly points out: "As far as opinions of our center are concerned, the majority are impressed, but those who expect something spectacular are disappointed."

For some years now, mixed groups of Catholics and Lutherans from Germany have taken part in ecumenical meetings organized by the Focolare Movement at the Mariapolis Center of Rocca di Papa, near Rome. These offer further opportunities for deeper knowledge of one another's traditions. Dr. Fürst, who took part in such a meeting in May 1975, tells of his deepest impressions: "Naturally, I can only express my own personal views. For me, a high point was when we heard the meditations on the Word of Life, given by Chiara Lubich. Usually we think of the word of God as a series of declarations written in a book. What emerges so clearly from these meditations is that the word of God is a living reality because it is Christ. It is far greater and more dynamic than we can possibly imagine. But I was particularly struck by the definition of the word of life that was given: it is such precisely because it has to be lived. This really shook me because I am a preacher and, therefore, I proclaim the word of God. I realize very clearly that unless I lived the word, I would never have an effect on anyone.

"Another significant moment was the visit of Cardinal Willebrands. At this point I should mention that among Protestants there is always the fear that the great, powerful Catholic Church would like to crush the small, weak evangelical churches. At that meeting, members of the Free Churches were also present, and they felt this problem acutely. But the words of the Cardinal were so fatherly, so full of the Holy Spirit, that even these brothers were enthusiastic when I spoke to them afterwards. The Cardinal showed the church and Christianity in a much wider perspective than we had previously seen it.

"Finally, the Catholic Mass at the catacombs: it is always a very special event to be able to take part in the liturgy in these places where unity can almost be tangibly felt."

The result of such meetings and of the life at Ottmaring is a deeper comprehension of aspects of other traditions which in the past have been the cause of misunderstandings. Speaking from the Lutheran point of view, Dr. Fürst tells of his deepened awareness of the role of Mary: "The reformers themselves had a higher conception of Mary than those who came after them. I still find it difficult to understand devotion to Mary completely, but the concept the Focolarini have of her is becoming more and more my own. They stress the imitation of her life, of reliving as far as possible her mission, which is giving Christ to the world. This is my Mariology too. And in this kind of Mariology, I find no obstacle to unity."

As far as the future of Ottmaring is concerned, there is great hope. Dr. Fürst sees possible developments of other activities in different fields, such as the defense of the family, of youth, and of life, and a greater contribution to the specific field of ecumenism: "Mainly due to the action of the Focolarini in the movements like New Families, New Humanity, Gen, etc., something is already being done in these fields. Particularly with families and these other areas, I hope very much that more can be done. In our Brotherhood, to which many teachers belong, we are mainly involved in schools at present, working with the students.

"I am not a prophet, but my ideas on the future of Ottmaring are very much bound up with my faith (which is the reason why I moved here; it was certainly not just out of curiosity). But faith is always confirmed by outward signs from God, and I feel that these signs show that Ottmaring will grow. What I would hope is that this ecumenical experience will produce a contribution to the theological field, although obviously this must be a consequence of life."

So far, the experiment has met with steady and quiet success. Have there been problems, or is there a danger that difficulties will arise in the future so that the Catholics and Lutherans of Ottmaring will reach a deadlock as has been the case with so many ecumenical endeavors? Again, Dr. Fürst's reply is the answer of faith, a faith which is expressed as certainty: "In the two years I have lived at Ottmaring, I have seen the union between everyone grow tremendously, even though difficulties have not been lacking. But I would say, rather, that these very difficulties have helped to cement our bond: the cross remains the necessary condition for unity."

A Letter from Roger Schutz of Taizé

Over ten years ago, I received some young men and women in Taizé. I listened to them peacefully, and the more I listened to them, the more I discerned in them the light of Christ. I spoke to them of the local parish priest and of the difficulties that he encountered. And that was enough for them to show him their friendship and invite him to spend his holidays with them many times afterwards.

Who were these young people? The Focolarini.

After this occasion, we met many times, and not only in Taizé, but also in Rome, Florence, Milan, and elsewhere, and there was always the same light of Christ.

One day when I was in Rome, I invited Chiara Lubich, the one who founded the spiritual family of the Focolarini, to see me. That meeting with Chiara has left a deep impression on me. I saw her often afterwards, and I can say that the Gospel really shines through this woman.

Then I do not forget that Chiara was chosen from among the humble, the workers, so as to confuse the strong and powerful of this world. And I praise Christ, our Lord. I know that, through women like Chiara, God gives us an incomparable instrument of unity for us Christians who have been separated for centuries by a long divorce. Therefore, blessed be the poor in spirit, reconciled and unified through Jesus Christ.

Brother Roger,
Prior of Taizé, France

Contacts with the Orthodox . . .

The various meetings that took place in Istanbul between Patriarch Athenagoras and Chiara Lubich were of special value. Joyfully declaring himself to be a member of this Movement, Athenagoras was especially pleased by the fact that the witness of mutual charity unites all people, for it is not made only for a few who represent an interested élite. This is also corroborated by our experience of these years.

In Beirut, the leaders of the "Mouvement de la Jeunesse Ortodoxe" (MJC), one of the most active movements among Orthodox youth, are in close contact with the Movement. Bishop Georges Krodes, their founder, and presently the Metropolitan for Lebanon, encourages and follows this initiative closely.

In Regensburg, Germany, Bishop Graber has entrusted the "Regensburger Begegnungen" (Regensburg Encounters) to a group of Focolarine. The task of this center is cultural and artistic exchange with Eastern Orthodoxy, through meetings, trips, congresses, etc.

A large group of Orthodox follows the spirituality of the Movement in Cyprus, and the dialogue with the Orthodox has also developed in other nations.

During a gathering of Greek Orthodox and Catholics in Rome in April 1975, the following message was sent to the participants by His Holiness, the Ecumenical Patriarch Dimitrios I, successor of the great Patriarch Athenagoras:

> We bless with all our heart the meeting of Catholics and Orthodox in Rome, a meeting sponsored by the Focolare Movement. We are present with you in spirit. . . .
>
> In the midst of so many words and ideologies, our spiritual and religious life must be based on and inspired by the Word of God

in order to be genuine and authentic. Only in this way will our life be the framework within which we can fulfill our ardent desire to visibly form one body under one head, Jesus Christ, the Word of God.

This meeting, held in Rome in the Holy Year atmosphere of renewal and reconciliation, is of particular importance and significance. Renewal and reconciliation, as the fulfillment of the last prayer of Jesus, the Word of God, are based on living his word in general and this one in particular. For this reason there is not a better or more suitable time to deal with this theme than during this Holy Year.

Let us all be reconciled with God who loves all men . . . and let us announce to all our brothers that his love for man is so great that sooner or later he will grant reconciliation and perfect unity among us. This we believe most firmly.

. . . and with the Anglicans.

After the first contacts with Anglicans in Great Britain, the Archbishop of Canterbury received Chiara Lubich in London on the first day of July 1966. Archbishop Ramsey encouraged the Movement to work among the Anglicans and said that this spirituality focusing on unity "had a lot to offer to the Church of England." Since then, ecumenical meetings have also multiplied with other Christian churches.

Charity showed itself to be the light that dissipates many prejudices; it showed itself as the means of discovering the true values of each church and as an aid to unify different tendencies within the various denominations. Below, we have printed some questions asked of Doctor Dimitri Bregant, one of the leaders of the Focolare in Great Britain.

Q.: The ecumenical experience of the Focolare Movement is not limited to Ottmaring or to Germany. We could say something about it in almost every country in the world. The ecumenical contact of the Movement with the Anglicans in Great Britain is very interesting. Dr. Bregant, could you explain to us what this is all about?

Dr. Bregant: Since the beginning the characteristic of the Movement in Great Britain has been that it has offered its spirituality to both Catholics and Anglicans at the same time, and those who have embraced it have grown together. While they were both spiritually maturing, the first vocations in the Movement blossomed, both among the Catholics and among the Anglicans. At first, we did not know how the Movement should be structured there. We were wondering if each branch of the Movement should have two separate sections for Catholics and Anglicans. The common desire of remaining together prevailed. In England there is, therefore, one Movement with all its different branches as it is all over the world, but every branch is mixed. There are Anglican Focolarini who live in community with the Catholic Focolarini (even if they observe the prescriptions of their Church and its religious practices). Catholic and Anglican Volunteers work together, and so do the Gen.

The Focolare Movement in Great Britain was ecumenical from its beginning, but we never had any theological discussions between Catholics and Anglicans. Our relationship from the beginning was based on the Gospel and it has been a concrete experience that precluded discussions about differences.

Q.: Is it possible to live together without resolving differences?

Dr. Bregant: Others have asked this question. It is not that we did not see the differences from the beginning or that we did not want to mention them or that we try to hide them. We were always aware of and accepted the differences and often with a great suffering because the more our life — based on a daily concrete experience — grew, the more evident it became that there is a separation. This separation was consumed by charity, which became the cement of unity among us all; for this reason we were never disappointed. Others who started the ecumenical dialogue in the hope of reaching an immediate solution of the problem, felt, as soon as the dialogue encountered a serious difficulty, that it was an insurmountable obstacle. For us, everything was based on personal experience, on the contribution of each one. From the unity built little by little, joy was derived because this unity was not something vague but something real and concrete since we were all aware of the fact that

there were differences. We also understood from the
beginning that those who have the grace to bring about a
complete unity are the two churches and not the Focolare or other movements. We will be able, however, to
offer our experience to those who have the task of
solving the theological problems. We know we can start
now to give our contribution by showing that it is possible to grow in the same reality of life while remaining
faithful to our respective churches and following their
religious practices.

**An Address by the Right Reverend Thomas A. Fraser,
Bishop of the Episcopal Diocese of North Carolina, to the
Ecumenical Mariapolis of Greensboro, N.C., May 14, 1976.**

In 1972, I spent some time in Europe. My major task
was pursuing and investigating two areas — the one, Anglican
and Roman Catholic relations, and, the second, a personal
pursuit which I had been struggling with for many, many
years and which I put under the title of "The Church
and Culture."

These two pusuits took me to Oxford, Cambridge,
King's College, Louvain, to the Dominicans at St. Mat-
thias in Trier, and on into Italy. I had explored my
subjects with academicians and clergy. A month later I
was in Rome at the Anglican Center — which is known

April 1976. Roman Catholic—Anglican Convention at the International Mariapolis Center in Rome, Italy. *Above:* The Archdeacon of Canterbury (England) Bernard Pawley participating in the meeting. *Below:* The Auxiliary bishop of the Anglican diocese of Manchester, England, Edward Wickham, with his wife, in St. Peter's Square, after an audience with the Pope on the occasion of the same ecumenical meeting.

Above: **The Right Reverend Thomas A. Frazer,** Episcopal Bishop of North Carolina, speaking at the Ecumenical meeting in Greensboro, N. C. sponsored by the Focolare.
Below: A partial view of the audience.

to us as the Anglican presence in Rome. It is kind of a bridge between the Anglican Church and the Roman Church at the Vatican. One afternoon I was introduced to a young priest and a very interesting lady who came for tea. (I was not supposed to be there, I just happened to be there.) And in the course of our conversation, they asked what I was doing. I told them that I was investigating Anglican/Roman Catholic relations, and the Church and Culture which, in simple English, meant: How can you be what you are and be a Christian? The lady looked at me with very piercing eyes and she wanted to know whom I had asked this question, and I said, "Oh, I've tried this one on clergy, and principals of colleges, and monastics, and I've been trying it on myself for a long time." Then I said, "Tell me, what do you do?" She said, "I'm a doctor." I said, "Well, to put it very simply, how can you be a doctor and be a Christian?" She kind of passed it off and continued the conversation on where I had been and whom I had talked to, and what we had talked about; and, finally, I said, "Well, you know, Dr. Fallacara, the basic question is to myself, 'How can I be a bishop and be a Christian?' But, tell me, how can you be a medical doctor and be a Christian?" And, I guess, I will never forget her eyes. I felt as though she was looking straight through me. She said, "Do you really want to know?" I said, "Yes!"

And this simple question led us into a conversation of several hours in which she told me a story to which I listened very carefully. It was the story of four girls in

World War II, in northern Italy. (You will probably hear a great deal more about this story as your time goes on.) Then she put the question to me as to whether I could find Christ in my fellowman. And I said, "Oh, for me this is very difficult." I said, "You don't know some of the people that I know." She continued to pursue this finding Christ in your brother.

Well, that afternoon started a long pilgrimage for me. Every afternoon, at about three o'clock, I would end up in her office where I was introduced to a very fascinating person whom I love and respect greatly — Igino Giordani, who is in the Ecumenical Office in Rome. I met with them almost three or four afternoons a week and they gave me their time understandingly and I kept asking questions, and asking questions.

One afternoon I said to Igino, "Igino, you know, this is all a matter of the heart but not of the mind, and this bothers me. I am a man of mind, I am a man of reason." And I will never forget how Igino looked at me and with the most loving voice said, "Bishop, let your heart rule your mind!"

I became more interested in the Movement and finally learned about a place called Loppiano, and I asked, "Can I go to Loppiano?" My time in Italy was running out and this was just before Holy Week. Dr. Gabri Fallacara said, "Well, I'll see if we can arrange this."

I spent twenty-four hours in Loppiano, I know they were glad when I left because we stayed up until two o'clock in the morning and got up at five o'clock the same morning, and they said, "Have you got any more questions?"

I met with the 400 young people who were there at Loppiano and I must say that it was an experience that I will never forget. I have never experienced being with 400 young people of every nation, every race, every tongue, and not being conscious of any differences — they call it Loppiano, they ought to call it "The City of Love."

I returned to Rome and had the opportunity to have an audience with His Holiness Pope Paul. He was interested in what I had been doing. He was very kind and very gracious, and very warm. Finally, I told him that I had met the Focolare Movement. His eyes brightened and with a smile on his face, he spoke in the most wonderful terms of the effort being made by the Focolare Movement to live the Gospel of Love.

This has been my experience and my introduction to the Focolare Movement during Lent 1972. This past week I received a very cordial and loving letter from Igino Giordani and Gabri Fallacara in which they spoke of the efforts of people and the interest of people in the Movement in this area and sent their love and Unity to all who were involved.

I want to express my appreciation to Bishop Begley* for being present and also to Father Nuzzo and Sharry, Joseph, and all the rest who have brought to me a sense of the Unity of the Movement and have been gracious enough to meet with us here in Greensboro.

*The Roman Catholic Bishop of Charlotte, N.C.

12. THE SUMMER MARIAPOLIS

One of the largest and most typical gatherings sponsored by the Focolare Movement is the Mariapolis, which takes place each summer in many parts of the world. The Mariapolis is a temporary "city" composed of hundreds and, sometimes, thousands of people of all classes, ages, and vocations who gather together to experience a new type of relationship based on the Gospel law of love. The participants are invited to live with total love for one another just as Mary, the prototype of Christians, did for Jesus. This is why it is called "Mariapolis" or City of Mary.

The burst of life that this kind of communitarian witness brings about is demonstrated by the impressive and ever-growing number of young people who come each year to participate, and also by the effects of the Mariapolis: For many, living in the Mariapolis means a deep inner conversion, a decisive experience for changing or renewing their living habits, a rediscovery of Christianity, and a clear-cut choice of God.

This original experiment of a Christian community coming together temporarily had its beginning in 1949. That year, the first Focolarine and Focolarini gathered together with Chiara Lubich in a small village of Tonadico, in the Italian Alps, in a climate of very profound spiritual unity. For the next ten years, the temporary "City of Mary" took place each summer in the valleys of

Fiera di Primiero in northern Italy. This mountain village became the cradle of the first Mariapolis in 1949. The lives of thousands of people changed here during the eight Mariapolises which took place each July and August until 1959.

Mariapolis takes place all over the world. *Above:* Part of the 500 participants at Na-Trang Mariapolis in South Vietnam in 1974.
Left: A Mariapolis in the Cameroons, Africa.
Below: A moment of recreation during a Mariapolis in France.

Different views of the North American Mariapolis in Loretto, Pa., in 1975.

the Dolomite Mountains, growing both in number and in the variety of the groups present. It reached a peak in 1959 when those who passed some time in that ideal city numbered more than ten thousand persons from twenty-seven different nations. Among them were priests, religious of many orders and congregations, as well as many bishops. Since that date, Mariapolises have been held in many locations around the world; presently, about thirty are held every year, in all of the continents.

The following are some impressions of participants in the different Mariapolises.

A mother: "I understand here that at the end of my life there is going to be only God and me. I want to start right away to live this awareness, to choose him now."

A construction worker: "I never found happiness in my life. I didn't even know what it was. There was such emptiness, such sadness, such anger in me that I ended up rebelling against God. I hadn't been to church for fourteen years. But here, while I was seeking love, I learned that love means to give love, not to receive it; to receive it is a consequence. Here I also learned a lesson in humility. In the dorms near me there was a handicapped person. I saw how people were washing his feet and taking care of him. Their simplicity destroyed my pride. I couldn't sleep all night. The following day, with my knees shaking, I went to confession. I understood that suffering is Christ, and he is happiness."

A student: "I thought that to have an apostolate

meant to speak or preach, but today I understood its essence. Words will pass, sermons will go, but charity will never pass. It is beautiful to think that a man can give God to other men in every moment of his life."

A housewife: "I lost my husband two years ago. He was killed in an accident. In the Mariapolis I found the strength to forgive those who were responsible for his death."

A couple from Africa: "We have realized that this ideal is the real African spirit which is open to the universal paternity of God. It opens up the closed mentality of the clan which too often destroys even the unity between husband and wife. It fully satisfies the African need for a family."

A Japanese Shintoist: "The real rapport among people that one finds in the Mariapolis tells me that beyond all religious differences there is only one God."

A former drug addict: "It's true that our society is putrid, but from now on I'll not walk the streets any more to escape. Instead I'll go to help the needy and the handicapped. . . . Here I have spent the most beautiful week of my life."

A blue-collar worker: "Here you either commit yourself or you run away. There is no in-between. You can feel how the Lord gives you the possibility of overcoming a cross when it comes. Now it's up to me to adhere always to this plan. I feel myself fulfilled in it, because I feel that it is the key to my whole life, to all my problems. . . In the factory there isn't any kind of real relationship among the workers or with the managers. We're not able to feel as brothers who are in the same boat. Now, when I get back to the factory, it'll no longer be a question of merely finding suffering. For now I can transform it into love, I can be a sign of contradiction, a person who knows how to give himself daily, without compromise, before God and his neighbors. Now, I'll be the one to look for new and real relationships."

A college student: "Today, I've discovered the Church in all its splendor. I have discovered it as a community of brothers, as a communion of material and spiritual goods. ... Here in the excellent rapport of this community, a person can find full freedom and can foresee the solution to the problem of communism and to selfish individualism."

13. LOPPIANO: A MARIAPOLIS WHICH LASTS FOREVER

"I wish the Mariapolis lasted forever."

At every Mariapolis, when the time of leaving approaches, the same words are repeated by many of the participants. It is an aspiration which goes back to the first Mariapolis of 1949. Even then Chiara Lubich and her first companions had said, "There will be a city one day which is a full and complete expression of our Ideal." And the city was conceived as a modern city with schools and industries. Its name would be "Permanent Mariapolis." There were several steps taken before the city could become a reality.

In 1962 some young people coming from various continents had arrived in Italy with the desire of giving their lives to God and specifically of reliving an experience which seemed impossible to be relived, the experience of the beginning of the Focolare Movement. Chiara and her first companions tell us that when the bombs of World War II were destroying everything all around them, it seemed that God himself was dropping some kind of spiritual bombs in their souls that would change their lives more radically than the bombs outside. Their previous ways of understanding life even though good, were transformed and united in an evangelical point of view that resulted in a new way of living.

Work did not seem any longer to be simply a way to make a living; it was seen as the performance of God's will.

Loppiano, Italy. *Above:* The original villa which housed the first group of young men who in 1964 started the Permanent Mariapolis. Now it houses the Art Center where about 60 young women work.
Below: On the left, one of the buildings where the young women live. On the right, an old farmhouse remodeled.

Loppiano, Italy. *Above:* The factory building now used as an auditorium to host the thousands of visitors who go to Loppiano.
Below: Sunday visitors in Loppiano: besides a visit to the different facilities, the program includes sharing of experiences and songs from the young people who live there. Most of the visitors are young.

At the same time, the spreading of the kingdom of God could not be limited to one's concern for a few hours a week, but had to be the expression of one's whole life.

Also the way of understanding sanctity changed. No longer could they consider an individualistic way of going to God through one's own separate practices of piety. They wanted first of all to seek the kingdom of God in their midst through charity, through mutual love. Sanctity would come then as the promised hundredfold, as the consequence of a life of charity which is the bond of perfection.

Even the physical well-being of each one of them could not be considered egotistically. It could not be wasted carelessly. Their health, they understood, had to be put at the service of God in their brothers, and this might at times be more of a penance than fasting or wearing hairshirts.

The same was true for every other aspect of life. For they discovered a new way of understanding how to study, how to keep the house, how to remain in touch with one another. It was a new, evangelical way of living.

The young people who came in the beginning and those who followed in subsequent years, wanted to repeat that experience, to be formed in a new school encompassing all facets of life and to acquire a Gospel mentality. They were going to be the seed of the future permanent Mariapolis.

Was It a Dream?

If today you happen to take a ride going south from Florence on the "Highway of the Sun," and exit at Incisa Valdarno and then climb the beautiful hills of Tuscany, you will find a dream that has become a reality. Suddenly, after a sharp turn of the road, the "permanent Mariapolis" appears: new houses, factories, large modern buildings, remodeled old farm houses. Everything that is new blends in well with the natural surroundings and the older buildings.

The permanent Mariapolis is also called Loppiano from the name of the locality where two hundred and fifty acres of farmland was given to the Focolare Movement in 1964. Since then it has been growing larger and more populous. Maybe it is still too small to be called a city, but it has all the characteristics of a city. You can find a large professional carpenter shop as well as a "mini-market." You can also find a very advanced recording studio, used by the "Gen Rosso," the well-known singing group of Loppiano, as well as a trailer industry. New buildings are being added constantly, and new streets are being built or enlarged. Families with their children are now living in Loppiano. It is amazing to see how well everything has been transformed, but it is not the buildings which make Loppiano a center of attraction for many.

The thousands of visitors who arrive at Loppiano from Europe and all over the world, are attracted by the unity

Loppiano, Italy. *Above:* The young men live in these modern prefabricated châlets. Their living together according to the spirit of the Focolare must have the characteristic of a family life, imbued by the supernatural rapport of continuous and mutual love.

Below: Previous chicken coops now form the industrial section of Loppiano where most of the young men work.

Loppiano, Italy. *Left:* Two of the young women of the Art
Center. The productions of the Center have been rewarded with
many international acknowledgements because of their high
artistic level.
Above: The Sculpture Studio. Ave Cerquetti, Director of the
Sculpture Department, working on a crucifix. Many of her
sculptures are now in churches and public squares in Europe
and South America.

Left: **Some of the young men** working as carpetlayers. This type of work puts them in contact with people from outside and the testimony of their unity while working often provokes questions and explanations. Many of these people end up in Loppiano for a visit, which most of the time is the beginning of something new in their lives.

Above: Other young men working on the assembly line of trailers.

Loppiano, Italy. Other types of work by which the young people of Loppiano support themselves.

that is achieved among the citizens with so many differences. The more than four hundred inhabitants come from forty-three countries and sharply different social backgrounds. Doctors, laborers, blacks, whites, and orientals live and work together. They seem to have nothing in common. Could there be any affinities, for instance, between Lo Kin Sang, a math professor from Hong Kong, and Lucero from Columbia, or between Theresa from Uganda and Franny from Chicago? It is difficult to imagine what interests could be shared by Ivanka from Yugoslavia and Marluce from Brazil, or by Jaga from the Philippines and Paul from the Ivory Coast.

There is a striking difference between Roswitha, a blond Lutheran girl from Germany, and the dark haired boy who comes from Spain with a very strong Catholic tradition. Michael, the young Irishman, has very little in common with Malcolm from England, and Peter from the United States with Jonyai from Thailand. Nevertheless they are one.

At Loppiano unity among races is a reality. These citizens are aware of being children of the same Father and they live like brothers.

A City on the Mountain

Young people flock here from all over the world in order to live a deep experience of Christianity when they study, when they work, and when they contemplate.

Even wealthy persons leave their comforts and come here to earn their daily bread by the sweat of their brow and to live together with people who are different because of their economic, racial, and cultural backgrounds. The joy which shines on the faces of those who live here is a joy which could never come from any kind of entertainment, nor from the most unrestrained pleasures. Unfortunately there is not enough space to accommodate the hundreds and hundreds of people whose requests to participate in this life have to be turned down every year.

What, then, is the real attraction of Loppiano? One answer surely can be found in these words of Jesus:

"You are the light of the world. A city set on a hill cannot be hidden. Men do not light a lamp and then put it under a bushel basket. They set it on a stand where it gives light to all in the house. In the same way your light must shine before men so that they may see goodness in your acts and give praise to your heavenly Father." (Matt. 5:14-16)

Loppiano Community of Workers

Work is very important in Loppiano. Work makes Loppiano a city, for it cannot be called a city without work. But here, to work is to do the will of God through a constant and at times painful and heavy effort. The inhabitants work together trying to maintain a rela-

The two international musical bands of Loppiano. Through their songs and records they have "exported" on the stages of many European cities, the revolution of life of which Loppiano wishes to be a living testimony.
Above: The "Gen Verde" band. *Below:* The "Gen Rosso" band.

Above: **The baptism** of the first-born of Rod Gorton from California and Mazia from Austria; they form one of the families living in Loppiano.

Prayer, the Sacraments, the daily celebration of the Eucharist are moments in which the people of Loppiano gather in order to live together their rapport with God.

Below: **Children in Loppiano** grow up with the awareness that it is possible to build a society based on the Gospel. They see it through their everyday life at home and through their participation in the life of the Mariapolis.

tionship of mutual love. They help each other to do everything with detachment and charity, and to show how powerful and luminous are all accomplishments when they are achieved through the presence of Jesus among men.

At Loppiano most of the citizens work for part of the day, and dedicate the other part to study at the International School of the city. Both production and study are greatly helped by the emphasis placed on working in unity. When they leave Loppiano, these temporary citizens are prepared to bring back to their own countries the human and Christian vision of the world which they have learned about and practiced here.

Sixty girls work at the "Ave Center" of arts and crafts which has several different sections. An important one which has almost become an industry is the ceramic department. The artists of the Ave Center have received many awards at exhibitions. Their sculptures and paintings are well-known in Italy and elsewhere. Behind the artistic production there is the same evangelical spirit which is at the basis of all activities. The artists share their individual ideas and inspirations. The outcome is often a new idea which is richer and more universal.

Thirty or forty girls design and manufacture women's clothes in a shop called "The Lillies of the Fields." New and quite elegant fashions are produced here. Their products bear witness to the beauty of God.

In "Campogiallo," a section of Loppiano, the young men mount trailers. When they first started they used to produce thirty a month and the production has gone as high as ninety a month. They work in small teams, mostly outside of Loppiano. The contact with other workers who have to install wiring or plumbing always leads to many questions, such as, "Have you done this all your lives?" "How come you are from so many different countries?" "How do you get along so well together?" After learning the answer, many end up increasing the crowds of Loppiano's Sunday visitors.

There are some important farming activities run by the Volunteers' Branch of the Movement. The Volunteers have started a farm cooperative and bought some adjacent land, bringing the entire extension of Loppiano to five hundred acres. This cooperative is totally based on the spirit of the Gospel. It is something daring and deeply Christian. The main products are olive oil and Chianti wine, which are among the best in the area.

The carpenter shop grows as the city grows. And there are other small activities, such as assembling water faucets and mounting hair dryers. All of the various jobs are necessary for the balance of the city's economy. However, progress in Loppiano depends upon the commitment that each person takes toward loving in a concrete way.

They say that in Loppiano one works as much in one day as others do in a full week. This is because the force behind everything is spiritual and of course the workers never go on strike. Why should they? They live together, program and plan everything together considering the possibilities and needs, and all are co-responsible for their

Loppiano. *Above:* **Convent of the White Sisters** founded by Chiara Lubich. They are contemplative sisters within the Focolare. *Below:* The sisters devote part of their time to work in order to support themselves.

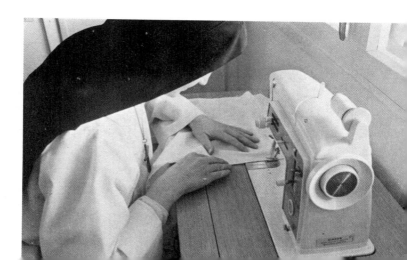

Right: **The parish church** of Loppiano with its eleventh-century bell-tower.

Below: **The Cooperative** of the Volunteers cultivates the land and produces wheat, olive oil, and wine.

city. One wonders if everything can always go so smoothly. Every once in a while there is a drop in production, they say, and it can often be attributed to a spiritual letdown. When the young people are all "up," the work goes well. On the other hand, when something happens which leads them to think of themselves instead of thinking of their brothers, work starts dropping off. It's a fact, "production in Loppiano is a thermometer of the spiritual life of the city."

Communion of goods

One of the leaders of Loppiano was recently asked how things are shared in the city. The following is his answer.

"We have certain jobs available here. To make a living the young people arriving join in to keep the little industries going. The jobs are different, however, and the profit varies according to the type of work involved, but we still keep all the different activities going. To limit ourselves to only one, even if lucrative, wouldn't be wise, for the outside companies offering us the work can change their minds or have problems themselves. Even if the profit made is different in the different shops, each individual wants to work to the fullest of his ability. And then he gives to the common fund whatever he earns and receives all he needs.

"What is all he needs?" We asked.

Needs differ from person to person. But in general he will have one suit and not two if all have one, two and not three if all have two. The sharing makes it possible for everyone to have what he needs.

The next question then is this: "If production grows and things go well, will you reach the point where the city is rich and people can all afford, for instance, four or five suits?"

The answer is, "No way. If we make money in order to make ends meet, that's enough.

Up to now the houses and roads have all been built with money which divine Providence sent us in different ways. But there is still so much to be built. There are many, many young people who would like to come and live in Loppiano for a while but we have no room for them. We are very few when you think of the many who would like to come.

Furthermore, the Movement we belong to is not limited to Loppiano only. It's all over the world and all together we carry the problems, including the financial burdens, also of those whom we do not see."

14. FONTEM AND AFRICA

In continents other than Africa the Movement contributes especially to spiritual renewal within the Christian world. Its presence in Africa, however, along with that of other Christian organizations, coincides with the very presence of the Church, with the spreading of the Gospel. Those who meet the Movement there are often meeting Christianity for the first time. The question, therefore, is not that of bringing special structures or spiritualities but rather that of presenting purely and simply the life of the Gospel.

The African people, with their innate sense of tight social groups, warmly welcomed the spirit of community in the Focolare. At the same time, they were helped to overcome their tribal and racial barriers and to enlarge the dimensions of brotherhood beyond their tribes. This explains the vast spreading of the Movement in Africa. Initially, it was through the witness of missionaries who had met the Movement in Europe. Today the Focolare is known everywhere, from Zaire to Burundi, from Uganda to Central Africa, from Zambia to the Ivory Coast, Cameroon, etc. . . .

In Fontem, West Cameroon, a small city has been built up. Even though it is small in size, it has been of great help in providing a visible witness to the life of the Gospel. This city displays in the daily work of its citizens the values that the African, who is not bound by the abstract categories and values of the Western mind, is ready to receive.

This new city had its origins in an act of brotherly love towards a tribe, the Bangwa tribe, which was diminishing in number due to an extremely high mortality rate among the children. Some years ago a team of doctors, nurses and technicians who were all part of the Movement went to live with them. In time, a hospital was built and the serious mortality problem was solved. By working closely with the natives, the members of the Movement achieved a deep relationship of trust and brotherhood with them.

That was the beginning of the present small city with its hospital, schools, workshops, spiritual training centers for young people, and a church. In a few years the area has been transformed into a flourishing district of life and activity. This large complex might well be called the fruit of the Gen Movement, for in the past few years the Gen have helped the youth of many nations work together to raise the necessary funds and assistance for their "Operation Africa."

The small city of Fontem has become a center of interest and, increasingly, a place to visit for many young people of different countries. This, together with the mass evangelization which is taking place there demonstrates that Fontem is indeed a living example of the kind of witness Africa needs today. It is not a witness merely of individual Christians, or even of a small group; the variety of people forming the community of Fontem shows,

Above: **The Valley of Fontem,** West Cameroon. In ten years the forest has given way to a beautiful habitat where people like to make their homes. The silent and concrete witness of the Focolarini has contributed to the spreading of the Gospel here. Christianity in bringing development has incorporated the local traditional values. The people have greatly appreciated this and do not consider Christianity as something imported from another culture.

Below: **In this hut** the first two Focolarini doctors lived for more than one year when they started their medical aid to the Bangwa which led to the birth of the town of Fontem. The African Permanent Mariapolis mingles almost spontaneously with the local population.

Right: **Fontem, West Cameroon.** Some of the buildings of the academy which in a few years has become a focal point for the development of the region.

Young people from several African Countries go to Fontem attracted by the new kind of society they find there.

Above: **A mother** brings her baby to the maternity clinic for a check-up.
Below: **Fontem Hospital.** Here Vincent from Uganda has learned to be an analyst.

Right: **The hospital** was the first achievement made by the Focolare with the collaboration of the local people. It has enabled the Bangwa people to eliminate the high infant mortality rate which existed before. It was also the first nucleus of the international town of Fontem.

The new church of Fontem. The architecture blends with the
local environment and resembles a huge straw hut. The local
population has contributed much to its construction. Here Bishop Pius Awa of Buea, the diocese in which Fontem is located,
wanted to celebrate the liturgy of the closing of the Holy Year
1975 for his diocese.

through their unity, the incarnation of the Christian message in a way that words would never be able to express.

Moreover, since Fontem is becoming a center of formation in the spirit of unity that draws together young people from the whole continent of Africa, it seems to indicate that similar solutions should also work for the other continents of the world.

15. O'HIGGINS, A CITY OF HOPE

> *This is an interview with Mr. Victor Sabbione, who is responsible for the men's branch of the Focolare Movement in Argentina, Chile, Uruguay, Paraguay, and Bolivia. We were particularly impressed with Mr. Sabbione's account of O'Higgins, one of four little cities which are concrete social expressions of the spirituality of the Focolare Movement.*

Q.: Would you tell us something about the Movement in your part of the world and about O'Higgings in particular?

Mr. Sabbione: After an initial period of adjustment, we went through another period marked by many vocations. It was a time when a very large number of people totally consecrated their lives to God in the service of the Movement. These persons were the core, or better, the heart of the Movement. Soon after, in the mid-sixties, another period began. The spirituality of the Focolare spread at large. This coincided with an important moment in the history of Latin America which was marked by strong social, economic, and political changes, and by a very strong evolution in all areas, especially in cultural ones. The diffusion of the Movement brought us into contact with many people and made us aware not only of the problems in South America, but also of how these problems affect the mentality of its people.

We soon realized that something else had to be done. Watching the experience of the Movement in Europe with its many Focolare Centers, we saw that at the heart of all this life were such structures as the Mariapolis Center in Rocca di Papa and the permanent Mariapolis of Loppiano. The Mariapolis Center involved the spiritual formation of different people through brief courses held from time to time, while Loppiano provided for longer periods of formation which required a visible community, a "small city" capable of gradually transforming life around it. The need for such structures was felt more and more by all of us, even if the accomplishment of such ventures seemed disproportionate to our strength and means.

But, at a given moment, something happened which made us take an important step. A family told us, "On the outskirts of Buenos Aires we have a piece of land which is quite valuable, and we would like to donate it to the Movement so that something may be built there." This offering came as a complete surprise to us and made us consider seriously the building of a Mariapolis Center, even if it would not be easy. Overcoming our doubts, we went ahead and received a tremendous response from the people — including the very poor from the Andes Mountains. Within three years their contributions made it possible for us to construct housing for people taking courses of three to five days; this became our school for the formation of core groups in the different branches of the Movement. This building program was accomplished in spite of the fact that Argentina was in the midst of a very serious economic crisis.

Q.: Was it then that you thought of your permanent Mariapolis, a South American Loppiano?

Mr. Sabbione: No, not yet. But, while we were still busy with the Mariapolis Center and other projects, it happened that the bishop of Montevideo, Uruguay, who was in Rome for the Vatican Council, had an opportunity to visit Loppiano. He was so fascinated by it that upon his return to Uruguay, he contacted the Focolare in Montevideo and told them, "I have a piece of land about forty miles from here. There is also a little house which is old and in bad condition, but it is available. I put all this at your disposal so that you can start your permanent Mariapolis. There is a great need in Latin America for something which offers a concrete vision of a new society, even if it is on a small scale. We need a place which shows with facts that Christianity does not only transform the lives of individuals, but can change society too."

"We'll try," we answered. Shortly after this, a small group of three Focolarini and twelve Gen from Argentina, Uruguay, and Paraguay began their first experience. The isolated location of the land and especially the poor roads, which became inaccessible during winter and bad weather, caused our friends to spend a very rough year. They were often cut off from the outside world during the rainy season. These elements indicated that this was hardly the place for a permanent Mariapolis. On the other hand, in spite of the distance and the poor condition of the little house, our unquenchable spirit in forming this modest permanent Mariapolis stirred an enormous enthusiasm in the Movement. Many people, despite the poor roads and poor housing, after having visited the Mariapolis, asked to participate in our life. The young people especially were anxious to go there for a one-year course, knowing full well they would have to support themselves by tiresome farmwork. They were ready for a life which reminded us of the early settlers of the Far West. In paricular there were no mechanical implements for farming. Since the only means of transportation was the bicycle, nothing was motorized. The first donations that we were able to raise within the community went towards the repair of the roof, so that the rain would not drip inside, and towards the purchase of camp beds.

In spite of these difficulties, at the annual Mariapolis in Argentina the youth living there spoke with such force and conviction of their individual and collective experiences that at the end of the Mariapolis some members of the Capuchin order told us, "This is a marvelous thing, but you are in a very distant area where you have to build everything. We have a large, colonial style seminary with three wings, constructed during the 1930's, that is not being used. It is located only 160 miles from Buenos Aires, right in the center of Argentina and at the very heart of your zone. It is easily accessible to Paraguay and Uruguay. Fond memories prevent us from selling it, but we would like it to be used somehow for the Church."

As the superior of the Capuchin Order was not among those who spoke to us, we were not sure how much we could count on the offer. Later, however, the provincial superior came to invite us to see the land. When we approached the place, located about two and a half miles from the town of O'Higgins, our first impression was that it had been prepared for us by God. The property was well kept, cultivated, surrounded by a beautiful forest, and equipped with some agricultural machinery. I recall that as I entered the chapel, the phrase "Dominus vocabit me" (the Lord will call me) caught my attention.

We decided to transfer our permanent Mariapolis there. The land in Uruguay would be more appropriate for a small Mariapolis Center.

Q.: Would you tell me briefly the story of O'Higgins from its beginning until today?

Mr. Sabbione: At the beginning there were twelve of us. Immediately the number of young people began increasing. Our intention was clear and precise from the start: to create something that would be a testimony to a new life in every way, including the way to work. The way to work in these surroundings was to start transforming the extensive property into a fully cultivated farm. We fought big battles with insects and weeds in order to cultivate every piece of land. Besides the physical effort, we had to learn many new things about farming. All of this created a new unity among us which taught us to bring our spirituality not only to our family and social relationships, but to our work relationships as well. We tried to do all our work in the light of our ideal and especially with "Jesus in our midst."

The first year we cultivated corn as the Capuchins had

O'Higgins-Permanent Mariapolis, Argentina. *Above:* The central building surrounded by the different factories at the heart of the 100 acre farmland. Part of the building is used as a hotel for the constant stream of people who visit the Mariapolis.
Below: Some of the buildings which house the young women and their activities: like a clothing industry and others. Those participating in the Permanent Mariapolises support themselves through their work and share with the others their income.

O'Higgins. Raising cattle is one of the activities of the young men.
Below: The farm has been transformed in such a way to become a pilot-farm, although modest in size.

previously done. One day a truck arrived carrying our first cow. It was a gift from the Salesians at a school one hundred miles away. Taking this as a sign from God, the next year we reduced our corn crop and decided to start raising cattle too. We bought a few more cows and bred others. We now have twenty eight. Since we had a Focolarino from Switzerland who had experience in making cheese, we borrowed a copper pot from a Benedictine monastery over a hundred miles away and started a cheese industry. It seemed that everything was going well. What we had left over in the way of cheese and milk allowed us to start raising pigs. Afterwards, we also began raising chickens and now have a model chicken farm.

One of the young men who was a carpenter, began repairing and making furniture for the long-abandoned main building. Although he began with very primitive tools, one thing led to another until now in O'Higgins we have a magnificent carpentry shop. When we received a small jeep and then a large truck, we also started a car repair shop which has grown since.

Even though the youth attending our school of formation had increased to forty students, we felt that a Mariapolis was not really a Mariapolis if it were only a school. It must provide the opportunity for other interested persons to stay with us for some time in order to share our life. We needed to house them, and God had given us a building precisely for that. First we put mattresses on the floor in the vacant rooms. Later, little by little, half of the building was transformed into a residence for those who wanted to spend time with us. Now it can house well over two hundred people. During the summer, it is filled especially with the many families who spend their vacations at the Mariapolis. Also during the year its rooms are fully occupied by the many young people who come to visit. They come to rest, visit our different industries, and talk with us. They often speak about our spirituality, almost without our having to mention it.

The O'Higgins Mariapolis would not have been a real Mariapolis if the women's branch had not come to give it its full expression two years ago. Three houses were built for them nearby, and a bigger building with a large kitchen, living room, attic, etc., is under construction to house the young women staying at O'Higgins for different periods of time.

We have also established a clothing industry, thanks to a large knitting machine that someone donated. We also have hundreds of beehives producing great quantities of honey. We plan to start an industry of sweets with the honey, peaches, and figs we produce.

Q.: You seem to have achieved fantastic growth. Can you give me some idea of the contribution made possible by the presence of a little "city" like O'Higgins to spreading the Gospel and to progress?

Mr. Sabbione: Keeping in mind that we are very small compared with the enormous South American continent, we have made a threefold contribution. The first is in the formation of youth — not only of those who spend a year with us, but also of those who come during the summer or during their vacations, or those who come only for two or three weeks. During these courses the young people find themselves involved in a very intense life, not only of classes but also of work. They share every aspect of our life.

The second contribution is the influence exerted by O'Higgins on other people who have participated in our lives for even a very brief period of time. We have created such a permanent bond with them that even if we never see them again, they would find it very difficult to lose the O'Higgins experiénce completely.

Our third contribution is an indirect one. Regardless of whether they have been at O'Higgins or not, many people in Latin America know of the existence of this permanent Mariapolis and of its significance. This is not because we have sought publicity. For instance, it has happened, often without our knowing it, that journalists who visited O'Higgins wrote about it afterwards, even in such well-known South American newspapers and magazines as *La Nacion* and *Panorama.*

Regarding our contribution to progress, well, I think it is impossible for Christians in any part of the world not to participate in progress, but more so in Latin America than in any other place. The Mariapolis of O'Higgins is a visible example of this intention lived moment by moment. It is a living example which has become more and more important in these last few years as the southern portion of Latin America has shifted from a feeling of optimism and confidence to a very negative feeling of hopelessness and pessimism. In the midst of this hopelessness O'Higgins remains a City of Hope.

16. THE FOCOLARE MOVEMENT AND THE CHURCH

The following interview concludes the series with the Focolare Movement. At Rocca di Papa, near Rome, I met Father Pascal Foresi, the ecclesiastical assistant of the Movement and the first Focolarino to be ordained a priest. I asked him to tell me something about the relationship between the Church and the Focolare Movement from its beginning to the present.

Q.: As a result of interviews with different members of the Focolare Movement, we have learned many meaningful details about the history of this Movement within the Church since its beginnings. Nothing was mentioned, however, in any of the interviews, about the difficulties that it encountered in becoming an integral part of the Church, even if we know well that the Movement has always proved itself to be faithful and obedient to the Church. Can you tell us, since you are the ecclesiastical assistant, if there were any difficulties and, if so, what they were?

Fr. Foresi: This question is a little difficult, since everything which is new always encounters some difficulties in becoming a part of a pre-existing society. I have to say, however, that even if we had to go through a lot of suffering, the "real" authority of the Church — not intermediary groups and commissions — always blessed and encouraged us.

At a time when the Movement was present only in the city of Trent, the Archbishop, Carlo De Ferrari, immediately gave it his blessing. On May 1, 1947, he approved it juridically in his diocese

Later on, when the Movement spread to Rome, new problems arose which came under the jurisdiction of the then existing Holy Office. But on May 21, 1953, Pope Pius XII received the Movement's foundress, Chiara Lubich, together with some representatives of the men's and women's branches in order to give them his blessing and to reassure them.

The thought of that audience still deeply moves me. That audience, although not confidential, was not made known to the public. It was not mentioned, in fact, by the Vatican press. It had been Msgr. Giovanni Battista Montini, then Pro-Secretary of State of the Vatican, who had sought this audience with the Holy Father for us, since he had a great esteem for the Movement.

While it seemed officially that we were only being studied by the Holy Office, Pius XII was giving us, through this audience, his encouragement and blessing. Later on, at a Bishops' Conference in 1960, some questions were raised about the Focolare Movement. Pope John XXIII then appointed a papal commission to oversee our progress towards officially becoming a part of the Church. The commission fulfilled its task, and on March 23, 1962, we were officially and publicly approved by Pope John XXIII.

This is not to say, however, that we did not suffer

Left: **Archbishop Carlo De Ferrari** of Trent (Italy) was the first one to bless the Focolare Movement and on May 1st, 1947 gave it canonical approval. At that time the Focolare was spread only in his diocese.

Right: **Pope Pius XII,** on May 21, 1953, received in audience the foundress and a group of members of the Focolare Movement in order to bless and encourage them when the Movement was not yet officially approved by the Church.

Below: **Pope John** appointed a commission in 1960 to study the place of the Focolare Movement in the Church. Under his pontificate, on March 23, 1962, the Movement was officially and publicly approved.

Pope Paul VI was still Monsignor Montini when he came in contact with the Focolare. He had the opportunity to know and appreciate the depth of its spirituality.
In the picture: The Pope speaks with Chiara Lubich who was leading 25,000 young people belonging to the Gen Movement in St. Peter's for the celebration of the Holy Year on March 2, 1975.

because of the uncertainties. And yet God had always sent someone among the higher authorities of the Church to reassure us and encourage us to go ahead. In reality, the Popes have never ceased in their encouragement of the Movement.

Unfortunately, so little is known about our history even in the more knowledgeable ecclesiastical circles that some still believe that we were approved after the Second Vatican Council by Pope Paul VI.

It is true that we have many reasons to be grateful to our present Holy Father. The official approval, however, at least verbally, goes back to Pius XII, and it was based on information received from Monsignor Montini and others. Pope Pius XII personally wanted this information to be completed. The official approval of Pope John XXIII came as a result of this initial act of courage and love on the part of Pius XII.

When Monsignor Montini became Pope Paul VI, he continued to show his great affection for the Movement, thus helping its development in a way which was unthought of before.

Q.: The Church, as well as humanity, is going through an historical period of unrest. Father Foresi, what is the role of the Focolare Movement in this unrest in the Church today? What do you think its task is for the future?

Fr. Foresi: In addition to what we know about this crisis, there are many publications which have described it in great detail. Paul VI has pointed out something about the negative aspects of it and certainly they can be easily recognized. He noted that thousands of priests and religious have asked to be laicized and that there is both a lack of vocations and a destructive criticism which, for some, has become a way of life. My impression, however, is that notwithstanding the negative elements, the crisis that the Church is going through today is leading it to a greater maturity.

This period reminds me of the years preceeding the fall of the Papal State. Then, too, many Catholics as well as anticlerics thought that the Church was coming to an end. A few decades later, however, they saw that the conquest of Rome in 1870 was in reality a leberation for the papacy.

The present crisis, of course, does not involve exclusively political and temporal issues as it did then. Today, there are theological and moral values at stake. I do not believe, however, that the real spiritual values will disappear as a result of this crisis, but only those entirely human elements, which might have been necessary to sustain the life of the Church up to now but which are not eternal. In fact, these human supports are what this crisis is all about.

Moreover, there is no real crisis about authority as such. The crisis involves a certain kind of authority. Just as in the question of the priesthood, the crisis is not about the priesthood itself, but about a certain way of understanding the priesthood. Neither is there a real crisis about penance, but only in the understanding of the sacrament of reconciliation. The crisis that exists in the family is bound to an authoritarian, paternalistic misconception of it, and not to the idea of the Christian family. This crisis in the family, however, could lead people to a deeper understanding of the true family vocation, and to a new way of perceiving the Christian community and mankind.

In conclusion, I certainly do not believe that the Church is coming to an end. The Church is from God and it will remain forever. It is only the human trimmings that are collapsing, and in the midst of all this confusion, it only appears that eternal values are also being hindered.

What is the role of the Focolare Movement at this moment? The Movement can and must be a part of today's Church, enduring the same sufferings and risks, putting into relief the essential values of the spirit and helping others to understand that what is now disappearing, in reality had already died.

Pope Paul and the Focolare Movement

In 1953, as we said, when Monsignor Montini was Pro-Secretary of State for the Vatican, he requested an audience with Pope Pius XII for Chiara Lubich and some representatives of the Movement. When he became Pope Paul VI, he continued to bless and encourage the Movement, thus helping its development in a way which was

unthought of previously. The following address was direct-
ed to a group of Volunteers of the Movement present at
a General Audience on Wednesday, January 15, 1975:

"It is certainly superfluous to explain what the Focolare means. It is a Movement which began during and
after the Second World War, and is made up of young
people who have decided to live the Christian life with
ardor, enthusiasm, and a great communitarian spirit. Once
more, we are happy to meet and bless them.

We want you, members of the Focolare Movement, to
know that the Church holds you in high esteem, that it
encourages you, and that it finds new hope in your
achievement within the Church, because you are not only
from Italy, but you are now international and, I would
say, spread throughout the entire Catholic world.

May God bless this new form of communitarian life,
this new Christian life and fervor which is blossoming in
the bosom of the Church, in spite of the crisis which it
is going through as far as communitarian forms of life are
concerned.

We repeat once more, we are pleased with you. We
have faith in you; you have all our best wishes and, God
willing, the continous and operative effects of our
Apostolic Blessing."

17. THE FOCOLARE IN NORTH AMERICA

It was certainly God's plan, and not any man's, that first led the Focolare to North America in 1960. Before this, only a few people scattered around this continent had ever heard of the Focolare. Somehow a small magazine published by the Movement in other English-speaking countries, had reached North America and happened to be picked up by a woman in Detroit, Mrs. Julia Conley, who immediately became interested in the Ideal it presented. She then found some priests who had met the Movement abroad and they advised her to take a trip to Europe herself if she wanted to know more. She went just in time to take part in a convention which was taking place in Fribourg, Switzerland, in August. The meetings were conducted in French and in German with simultaneous translations in Italian, Spanish, and Dutch. She was the only English-speaking person there. But someone took care of her and made sure she was always accompanied by her own personal translator. So much did she like what she found there that she wanted to bring the Movement back home somehow.

When Mrs. Conley came back to Detroit, she sent two tickets to the Center of the Movement in Rome so that two Focolarine could come to Detroit for a visit. In Rome they had the clear impression that God was pushing them more and more towards the United States. Since the Movement had already started in South America in

1958, and several Brazilians were even present at that Fribourg convention, how could they now refuse this invitation to North America which seemed to be providential? Thus, with hardly any time to prepare for their trip, two Focolarine came to the United States. Silvana Veronesi and Giovanna Vernuccio, both Italians, arrived with a little knowledge of English and, apparently, not much else. But they did come with the Ideal and with complete confidence in divine providence.

For a time the Focolarine stayed in Detroit, where they were the guests of Mrs. Conley. Then from there they started travelling almost all over the country, visiting many people who had been recommended to them by their European friends. Finally they landed in New York and found shelter in a basement in the Bronx. Since none of these places had a community of people who knew the Movement, the two women had to endure many hardships and to rely on providence along the way. It was quite an adventure.

After six months, they went back to Rome to make their report. Since they had learned to love the United States and its people and had seen the possibility and the need for the Focolare in North America, they convinced the Center in Rome to start a Focolare in New York City. Why New York? Perhaps it was because the Focolarine had made more contacts here. But, if one day an historian will write the full history of the Focolare in the United States, he will be obliged to conclude that it must have been caused by the mysterious plan of God.

Brooklyn, New York. Some of the Focolarini working for New City Press. The Movement has publishing houses in the U.S.A., Argentina, Austria, Brazil, Colombia, England, France, Germany, Holland, Hong Kong, Italy, Korea, Philippines, Spain, and Switzerland.

Chicago, McCormick Place. New City Press participating in the 1975 exhibit organized by the National Catholic Educational Association.

New York. *Above:* One of the offices of *Living City* magazine. *Below: Living City* is the bi-monthly magazine of the Focolare Movement in North America.

The official beginning of the Focolare in North America came on September 14, 1961, when two young women and one man landed in New York City. They were Giovanna Vernuccio, Sharry Silvi, and Antonio Petrilli. Giovanna and Sharry went to live in an apartment on Mulberry Street in Greenwich Village that someone had offered them temporarily. Antonio found a room at the Y.M.C.A. for a time. When the Englishman Joseph Patron joined him later, they moved into a little apartment in Queens. Sharry went to work at the United Nations, Joseph at the Paulist Press, and Giovanna and Antonio worked full time for the Movement. Thus, the first two American Focolari had started. There was no advertising, no fanfare—nothing was said to announce this new movement to New Yorkers. Usually the things of God do not make much noise.

Later, other Focolarini came from Europe. They all knew the hardships of starting out in a city like New York. What kept them going was a great faith in their Ideal. In an article published in *Living City* in 1970, Sharry Silvi gives a good account of how they felt: "Giovanna and I were riding on the subway. It was Friday night, near Broadway. Late that night people were coming and going, their faces said they were not coming from Church. So many of them. I was looking out the window but I could see nothing, only a dark wall. The subway was running fast. Giovanna was looking to the other side. We were sitting but many were standing all around us. Hundreds of people. What could the two of us do in this gigantic city? A feeling of discouragement almost captured me. Then we looked at each other. Giovanna was smiling. I smiled back. Two girls in New York — one would think we're nothing. And yet, with the grace of God and because of him, we were ready to die for one another. And we knew that Jesus could be present in the subways of New York, because of us — Jesus in the crowds of New York, in the apartment buildings and in the offices of New York. I was certain that that was where he wanted to be.

We went home with a great joy. New York was nothing in comparison to the power of the Almighty who has said, 'Where two or three. . .' New York seemed to be covered by the divine to such an extent that it never seemed the same to me again."

This faith and the continuous thirst for living with Jesus in the midst of them in the Focolare has created little by little what we call the "community" around the Focolare. It is made up of people who have been fascinated by Jesus living among two or three and have followed him. Truly the bond holding the community together has been the presence of Jesus among them.

On December 8, 1964, two young women opened the Focolare in Chicago. Starting out here was different, for a community that knew the Ideal was already in existence. For some time, Father Joe Scopa, a Chicago pastor who met the Movement in Italy, and some of his parishoners had been in contact with the Movement. Thus, when these Focolarine arrived, they found many things had been prepared for them, including an apartment that was

In New York, there are two schools of formation for both young men and young women who wish to become Focolarini. They spend one to two years in these schools where they deepen their knowledge of the Focolare spirituality and learn how to live it. Some of them work and others study and they share everything in order to support their communities.
In the picture, a group of girls who are in the school of formation.

Leaders of the Gen Movement, coming from various cities in North America, gather regularly in New York to renew their unity so that the same spirit might exist in each Gen group.

been prepared for them, including an apartment that was fully furnished and a pantry that was full of food. Then in the Spring of 1965 the Men's Focolare began too. And before long there came from Chicago the first American vocations to the Movement.

About the same time that the Chicago Focolare was beginning, the famous Cardinal Bea came from Rome to visit Cardinal Cushing in Boston and happened to tell him about the Movement. Cardinal Cushing was so interested that he entrusted Monsignor Edward Murray, Pastor of the Sacred Heart Church in Roslindale, to see to it that some Focolarini would come to Boston. It took a couple of years before the first Focolarino could be sent there in 1966. For about four months he was Monsignor Murray's guest. Then in September of the same year, another Focolarino arrived and they began to live in the Focolare. Also, since 1974 there has been a Women's Focolare in Boston too.

From their home bases in New York, Chicago, and Boston, the Focolarini have over the years kept in contact with the people who knew the Movement and wanted to live its spirituality. These people came from several cities in New Jersey, from Philadelphia, Detroit, and even from Toronto, Canada. In 1965 a Women's Focolare was established in Toronto, and the Men's opened in 1968.

During this time several young people and some married persons felt the call to become Focolarini. Soon the first American Focolarini started crossing the ocean in order to go to Loppiano for their two years of training. Today American women and men are found living in the Focolari in Australia, Korea, Italy, Sweden, and England. Thus, the Americans can help to keep each Focolare an international home, which also provides an important witness to unity.

Around this first structure of the Movement — the Focolare, with its consecrated lay people — all the other different structures of the Movement came to life: the men and women Volunteers, the Gen, the New Families Movement, and so on.

In Chicago a Mariapolis Center has been created for all kinds of meetings of the Movement. It also has facilities for people to come together for weekends.

The bimonthly magazine *Living City* and the newsletter "Focolare News" reach thousands of people all over the country. And the publishing house called New City Press, although still small in size, serves the needs of the people who wish to know more about the Movements's spirituality.

At the same time, the Movement has spread also to places where the Focolare doesn't exist yet. The ways of God are infinite and we have seen how he reveals his ways when the right moment arrives.

Nobody ever thought of going to Texas since the Movement was mainly spread in the East Coast and in the Middle West, near the cities where the Focolare centers are located. But one day in San Antonio, Texas, the Mother Provincial of the Sisters of the Sacred Heart, Sister Mary Claude, received a letter from her Mother

Chicago, Mariapolis Center. Weekends and three, four, and five-day meetings are regularly held here for the different branches and mass movements of the Focolare.

The Movement has spread in North America among people from many different backgrounds. Living the spirituality brings a new dimension in their activities and creates among all a strong bond of unity which makes them a family. . .

. . . coming from as far north as Vancouver, Canada (above) or from as far south as Brownsville, Texas (below).

Sister Mary Claude, received a letter from her Mother General inviting her to go to Rome to take part in a meeting for sisters. Sister Mary Claude wrote back asking if it was really important for her to go since it was such a long trip and her occupations at home were many. The Mother General answered simply: "Let me know when you will be arriving." Sister Mary Claude went, of course. She came back enriched by an experience she wanted to share with all her sisters. Thus, she invited the Focolarine to San Antonio. Once there, many other people came to know the spirituality of the Movement. Now the Focolarine travel regularly from New York to San Antonio to keep in touch with the community born there, a community which has extended to the borders of the Rio Grande River.

We have published in a different section of this book the beautiful testimony of Right Reverend Thomas A. Fraser, Episcopal Bishop of North Carolina. It was through him that the Movement started there. Now the New York Focolarini and Focolarine go to Greensboro, North Carolina, every three weeks to meet with the community and to share experiences with them about the monthly word of life. This community is growing eccumenical because after the Episcopalians, the Roman Catholics have also gotten to know our spirituality.

In Montreal, several people had already heard about the Movement even before 1966. But in 1972 a young priest saw a pamphlet on the Movement in a wastepaper basket in his rectory. Out of curiosity he took a look at it. He liked the contents and wrote to Toronto, A few days liked the contents and wrote to Toronto. A few days later a Focolarino happened to be in Montreal and visited him. It was the beginning of a new center of activity for the Movement.

We could tell a lot of stories like this. A family moved from Long Island to Lebanon, Indiana. They knew that their task was not to talk about the Movement but to live its spirit. After one year several other families now get together with them to go in depth and to grow in the spirituality; and these people are not only from Lebanon, but also from nearby cities.

A Capuchin priest from Wisconsin, Fr. Bill Alcuin, during a trip to Italy in 1975 spent one day in Loppiano. Immediately he started dreaming about a North American Loppiano. When he returned home, he wanted to know more about the spirituality of the Movement. At the end of December 1975, he had the opportunity to be exposed to it in a four-day meeting with other religious at the Mariapolis Center in Chicago. Afterwards he made some plans to spread the Movement in his state and shared them with the Focolarini, who agreed with them. Hoping to reach all his many friends who were waiting for something like this Ideal, he took a Focolarino with him for five days in Wisconsin. They visited a lot of people and communities. And a second trip of four days followed almost immediately afterwards. Before long, people from Wisconsin started coming to visit the Focolari in Chicago. Thus, the spirit of Unity of the Focolare had found another new province.

Similar stories could be repeated for other places, such

as St. Louis, San José, Minneapolis, Washington, D.C., and Philadelphia; but it would take too long to tell them all.

Still, we should add a few words about Canada. In Vancouver, a lady who had heard about the Movement in the Philippines, started talking about it to her friends. They wanted to do something and invited someone to come from the center in New York. After that first meeting, others have followed. A seed has been planted and it is growing and spreading. And why not mention other Canadian cities — Sault Ste. Marie, North-Bay, Calgary, Edmonton, Ottawa? It is always the same story: someone somehow begins to live the spirituality and then a little community starts. The Focolarini feel the responsibility to visit these different groups regularly, both out of love for the people who wish to grow in the Ideal and in order to maintain unity among all parts of the Movement.

The Mariapolis, the summer convention of the Focolare, draws together every year an average of one thousand people coming from almost every part of the continent. It is amazing to see how the Spirit works. These people spend five days together and when they leave a new reality is born in them and among them. Thus, each Mariapolis becomes the beginning of a new growth of the Ideal. The life of the people who keep living its spirit becomes a light for others. They are causing a silent but constant spreading of the spirituality in North America.

At the end of a "youth day" sponsored by the Gen in New York in March, 1976, some young people said,

"This spirit is made for America." We were happy to hear this. It confirmed what Chiara Lubich said during her first visit to the United States in 1964: "I have visited many nations in Europe and South America and also in Asia, but this nation seems to me to be particularly ready for the spirit of the Movement."

18. Centers of the Focolare Movement

(Figures in parenthesis indicate the number of centers in each city.)

ALGERIA
Algiers (1), Tlemcen (1)

ARGENTINA
Berazategui (1), Buenos Aires (4), Córdoba (2), O'Higgins*

AUSTRALIA
Melbourne (3)

AUSTRIA
Jois (1), Linz (1), Salzburg (1), Vienna (3)

BELGIUM
Antwerp (1), Brugge (1), Brussels (3), Chaineux (1), Ingelmunster (1)

BRAZIL
Belém (2), Belo Horizonte (1), Fortaleza (1), Palmares (2), Pôrto Alegre (2), Recife (4), São Paulo (5)*

CAMEROON
Douala (2), Fontem (3)*

CANADA
Toronto (2)

CHILE
Santiago (1), Osorno (1)

COLOMBIA
Bogotá (2)

FRANCE
Albertville (1), Lille (1), Lyon (2), Nice (1), Paris (5), Toulouse (2)

GERMANY
Augsburg (1), Berlin (2), Cologne (2), Bexbach (1), Bonn (1), Heidelberg (2), Herten (1), Munich (6), Ottmaring, Regensburg (1), Stapelfeld (1), Steibis (1)

HONG KONG (3)

IRELAND
Dublin (3)

ITALY
Anagni (1), Ancona (2), Bari (2), Benevento (1), Bologna (2), Caltanissetta (1), Catania (2), Florence (2), Frascati (1), Gaeta (1) Genoa (4), Grottaferrata (12)**, Incisa Valdarno*, Lumarzo (1), Milan (8), Naples (3), Padua (4), Palermo (3), Reggio Calabria (2),

Rocca di Papa (6)**, Rome (15),
Romano Lombardo (1),
Syracuse (2), Turin (6), Trent (4),
Trieste (3), Vallo Torinese (1),
Vittoria (1), Zambana (1)

IVORY COAST
Man (2)

KOREA
Seoul (2), Kyong Ki Do (1)

LEBANON
Beirut (2)

NETHERLANDS
Amsterdam (2), Eindhoven (1),
Nijmegen (2),

PAKISTAN
Karachi (1)

PARAGUAY
Asunción (1)

PHILIPPINES
Manila (3)

PORTUGAL
Braga (1), Coruche (1), Lisbon (2)

SPAIN
Barcelona (2), Burgos (1),
Madrid (5), Murcia (1), Seville (2)

SWEDEN
Stockholm (2)

SWITZERLAND
Geneva (1), Zurich (8)

UNITED KINGDOM
Liverpool (2), London (4)

UNITED STATES
Boston (2), Chicago (5),
New York (6)

URUGUAY
Montevideo (2)

*Permanent Mariapolis
**International Centers